"Equal parts memoir and guidebook, *Open* offers exactly what it promises: wisdom (like water) poured out and into the cracks of our parched beings. Fischer paints pictures and spins stories that inspire us to be more curious, seek less perfection, and activate our flawed, human, yet still massive potential for the good of all people, especially those who've suffered from a lack of radically hospitable spaces."

—DOREEN DODGEN-MAGEE,
author of *Restart: Designing a Healthy Post Pandemic Life*

"Sara Fischer has written a modern adventure story of faith-in-action in our muddled, complex world. A page-turning saga of one woman's search for meaning, as well as her true calling, *Open* is soulful and witty, smart and captivating. Truly a tale to treasure."

—KAREN KARBO,
author of *In Praise of Difficult Women*

OPEN

OPEN

Adventures in Radical Hospitality

Sara Fischer

RESOURCE *Publications* · Eugene, Oregon

OPEN
Adventures in Radical Hospitality

Resource Publications
An Imprint of Wipf and Stock Publishers
199 W. 8th Ave., Suite 3
Eugene, OR 97401

www.wipfandstock.com

PAPERBACK ISBN: 978–1-6667–4589–4
HARDCOVER ISBN: 978–1-6667–4590–0
EBOOK ISBN: 978–1-6667–4591–7

AUGUST 16, 2022 9:43 AM

To the memory of my father,
who gifted me with his insatiable longing for justice,
and to my mother,
who has always helped me to see beauty.

To the Rahab's Sisters guests,
that they may know justice and see their own beauty.

Contents

Preface

*B*ecause *2020*. This micro phrase became increasingly popular as the year went on. You would see it in social media posts. At the end of business emails. I canceled my vacation three or four times, because 2020. For a year I pastored an Episcopal congregation with whom I had never worshiped in person, because 2020. Nightly protests against police brutality and in support of Black lives continued for hundreds of days, because 2020. In September, my city and the entire west coast was paralyzed for two weeks by unprecedented wildfires and hazardous air quality, because 2020. I watched friends and family members endure paralyzing anxiety and depression, because 2020. Companies like J.C. Penney and 24-Hour Fitness declared bankruptcy while Amazon got rich on scarcity: N95 masks, hand sanitizer, alcohol wipes, dumbbells, jigsaw puzzles, because 2020. I learned by trial and error to cut my own hair, because 2020.

A thick cloud of calamity and dread lay on top of my own mid-life questions of purpose. I needed good news, and I found it in the form of radical hospitality. The phrase "radical hospitality" has been around for a long time, and radical hospitality has shaped and formed me over decades like ocean on stone. But in 2020, when the long season of lockdown showed me how *in*hospitable many of our systems always have been, even before a global pandemic, radical hospitality took on new meaning.

I found hope not just for my own local work as a clergyperson in a denomination that sometimes feels as ossified as the free market economy, but hope for the whole world.

Ironically, the year began as a hopeful one for me: I was about to return to a city I loved, begin a job I'd dreamed of, and live full-time with my beloved husband from whom I'd been commuting 180 miles each week. I'd made the hard-fought decision to leave behind a high-paying, high-visibility job at a prestigious Seattle church for a small, struggling Portland one. It was a hard decision to make because I loved that Seattle community. But when New Year's Day came, my heart felt lighter than it had for several years, and I had faith that the year to come would bring good with it.

Amid what has been called a moral reckoning for the United States, I found myself doing some reckoning of my own in the years leading up to 2020. I'd struggled with the same existential conflict faced by many people: how was I to do some good in the world? What mark, if any, was I to make? As the daughter of a Mayflower WASP and a Jewish Marxist, I fought an internal battle between security and revolution, between independence and community.

In mid-March, a clergy colleague invited me to a weekly on-line clergy get-together to share sermon preparation ideas. She named the group "Preaching in the time of Apocalypse." Because 2020.

"Apocalyptic" is a word I heard more in 2020 than ever before. The Greek word from which it translates is "unveiling," or "revelation." What, indeed, might be revealed in this year when we have had to learn new ways of being open to one another? What might be unveiled as circumstances continually offered new ways to connect with people in grave need?

Over the course of 2020, I encountered the mutual aid movement, Portland-style. Portland, long thought of as the "Portlandia" punchline, would become the epicenter of conflict, tragedy, and perseverance during the long season of uncertainty, and at times terror, that was 2020. The combination of pandemic, police violence, and unprecedented wildfires meant that Portlanders who might not have been considered vulnerable became so. The people who cared for them through mutual aid organizations were young, tenacious, idealistic, and smart, making ready connections between people in need and larger issues of economic and climate justice. COVID-19, the Black Lives Matter movement, wildfires, and a city shrouded in smoke—each of these called forth from people and organizations more support, more generosity, more invitation.

What was unveiled in this apocalyptic year was radical hospitality. In this unveiling I discovered that radical hospitality just might save the world. With each new disaster were new stories of groups and individuals that have much to teach the rest of us about being open in a world of closure, not just when there is a pandemic. These were the stories I needed to hear and the stories I needed to tell.

I needed hope and good news in 2020, and I found it in radical hospitality. While 2020 has receded into the past, the hope and good news of radical hospitality persists. Welcome in.

Acknowledgements

This book has been such a crazy long time in coming that some of the people mentioned here may not even remember the help they gave. But like every good work worth doing, the stories and memories I've collected here are a communal effort.

I am grateful to the "founding mothers" of Rahab's Sisters whose imagination caught fire and made something happen which continues to capture hearts of so many: Eleanor Applewhite-Terry, Marilyn Brown, Marla McGarry-Lawrence, Tracy LeBlanc, and Cindy Stadel.

A great assortment of people helped to birth the writing itself: Suzy Vitello, best coach-editor-cheerleader ever; Scott Gunn, Stephen Schneider, and Sarah Monroe, early readers; Melinda Crouchley, the quickest and most cheerful copyeditor I've ever met; and the wonderful folks at Wipf and Stock who made finally bringing this book into the world a breeze.

I've had many great teachers who both taught and modeled writing from a place of humanity, vulnerability, and good humor, including Charlie Moran, Karen Karbo, and Lee Montgomery. Week in and week out, Dan Kayon (RAMP Fitness in Portland) has taught me to get strong, stand up straight, and breathe deeply. I shudder to think where I'd be without that.

I will never forget the people in East London whose work planted the seeds for Rahab's Sisters, has shown up in multiple sermons over the years, and informed how I have always understood that odd animal we call "parish ministry." These include Brian Ralph and his East End colleagues, Rio and Angela from the Maze Marigold Project, and all the women who came out of the shadows behind Whitechapel Road to share sandwiches and teach me about community.

I am indebted to the people who have taught me and continue to teach me about harm reduction, which I have come to see as the highest way of valuing every human life: Jessica Camargo, Amanda Risser, and the wonderful folks who staff the needle exchange van at Saints Peter & Paul week after week.

I wish my father was around to help me learn about mutual aid but in his absence, thanks to the many teachers put in my path, especially Aaron Scott and Adrian Groedendyk.

I like to say that Jesus "put the *radical* in radical hospitality" but the people who have taught me the most about what that looks like are Joe Parker, Anneliese Davis, Molly Mattern, and the countless Rahab's Sisters guests whose names have been changed in this book but whose stories continue to teach and inspire.

While the central work and message of Jesus was to unveil an alternative community where the poor and outcast have good news preached to them and share that good news with others, in the the present time that work itself is marginalized even within the institutional church that claims Jesus as its founder. Much of what I write about in this book would not be possible without mentors like Mark MacDonald, who will always be my priest, and Ken Leech, who I imagine is causing trouble in the next life as I write these words in this one.

I am grateful to the people of St. Paul's, Seattle, who pray the *Magnificat* every day and who spurred me to do the work that finally (*finally*!) gave birth to this book, and to the people of Saints Peter & Paul who made me their "pandemic priest" and who continue to say yes to radical hospitality with radical hope. And I am grateful to Christy, who never forgets to ring the bell.

I can't do much in life without my tribe of family and friends, many of whom occasionally scratched their heads about what I was doing with this book but never stopped believing. And last but never least, my guys, Mark and Nathan, who are both my heartbeat and my heart.

Chapter 1

Preaching to the Camera

"Don't go on too long, okay?" My husband's eyes twinkled over his mask as he spoke. "I'm not sure how long I can hold my arms like this."

I was about to preach a sermon in the tired little sanctuary of my new church, Saints Peter & Paul Episcopal Church in Southeast Portland, Oregon. But instead of addressing a small rag-tag group of Jesus followers, the smallest crowd I'd preached a Sunday sermon to in a very long time, I was preaching to my smartphone, held in Mark's two hands, his elbows bent to hold the camera at eye level.

The church was empty, save for me, Mark, a piano player, and two singers in choir chairs ten feet apart from each other.

"God comes to us in the flesh," I said into the camera. "And is raised in a fleshy body. Not just that, but he is raised with his wounds. This is good news for us who have bodies. And especially good news for those of us who have wounded bodies."

I stood on an X made with blue painter's tape, marking the trial-and-error tested distance between me and the camera. I stood there with some wounds of my own. I had just left a job and a city which had chewed up bits of my spirit and spat them out during a challenging couple of years when my day-to-day work was at odds with who I thought I was.

The people at my Seattle church were as lovely as the recently remodeled multimillion dollar physical plant they worshipped in, but I became restless after a couple of years. I had loved the worship space, the music, the incense, and the long silences that made the liturgy contemplative as well as inspiring. But the disconnect I experienced between the church and the very poor, whom I thought we were supposed to be helping, was painful, especially during fundraising season. I remember one Sunday afternoon curled up like a hedgehog in my Seattle condo, crying that I didn't want to be working so hard to fund a budget when the lion's share would go to my huge salary.

I emerged from that job intact, but the wounds to my integrity were closer to the surface than they might have been if I'd been able to start my new job with a little more fanfare. Everything was shut down because of the pandemic and there was no opportunity to greet my new parishioners in person. However, the church building itself was familiar to me. Over the previous, years I'd spent many Friday nights in its fellowship hall working for Rahab's Sisters, the long-standing outreach to women that kept me coming back again and again. I'd been there on Sunday mornings as a substitute from time to time when I was between jobs in 2015 and was grateful to be back.

I stood on a battered floor, damaged over the years by several failed experiments in recent decades with unbolting pews to move them around, attempts to make the space more inviting. The floor was linoleum over concrete and the walls were tired pine. The lights were traditional mid-century hanging cylinders, too high up to offer warmth with their glow. The pews, still intact, were traditional polished oak with a gentle curve at each end. Ironically, they might have been the most inviting thing about the physical space but removing pews had been a thing in the 2000s.

"God is present with us in our woundedness, no matter what. This is what we learn from the resurrection."

I read these words from my sermon's list of bullet points on a music stand in front of me. Each of the music stand's three legs also stood on bits of blue painter's tape, carefully marking the spot where the stand would be useful to me but out of view of the camera.

I didn't know, as I stood there, whether my congregation would be able to relate to this talk of wounded bodies and woundedness. I didn't know them well enough. For three weeks, I'd been live-streaming video over the Internet; I figured maybe a dozen souls were actually watching.

"Saint Irenaeus of Lyons reminds us that 'God became human, that we might become divine.'" Who knew whether this quote, a favorite of mine from a second-century Christian martyr, would land with the people I'd never met?

I had met five of them when I interviewed for the job in early January 2020. I arrived at the church on a Thursday evening. Like most churches, the true main entrance was the one in the parking lot up a couple steps that led to the kitchen, not the gated entrance on the other side of the block that led to the worship space. I also knew that there would be no doorbell or if there was one, from what I'd heard about the crumbling physical plant, it probably would not be working. So, I was glad to see through a window the interview team gathered around a table in the fellowship hall.

I knew Sharon, whose title of Senior Warden meant that she was second-in-command at the church, a volunteer lay leader who would be more eager than anyone to get a priest into the mix after a long vacancy. She and I had been in touch setting up the interview. The other four people were mostly familiar to me: two of them had been around other churches in the area and I knew them from my church consulting days; the other two were long-time members whom I hadn't formally met. They each had a copy of my résumé in front of them along with scraps of paper for notes.

"Well," Sharon said after introductions had been made, "I guess we should just start. Who wants to ask the first question?"

The group was silent for more than a moment. This was different from any interview I'd had.

"I'll start," said Linda, a retired office manager with soft curls framing her face, and bright blue eyes. "Some people come into churches and just fire the admin team. We have a good team. Will you keep them?"

Wow. Nothing like asking a challenging question right out of the gate. What was it about churches and changes? Lay leaders, the ones who most need to be open to a radical makeover, often hold on for dear life to everything as it is, or to a dream of things going back to how they once were in some glory day.

I told them I was so glad they had a good team and could not imagine "messing with success."

Oddly, after that first question, I remember very few of the actual questions they asked. The light in the room was pale fluorescent yellow, siphoned off by the dark outside the fellowship hall's many windows streaked with rain. It did not do kind things for the faces around the table, all midwinter pale and flat. They looked down at my résumé, asked their questions, took no notes.

"Why do you want to come here?" a woman named Mary asked.

The long answer would have been that having just turned sixty, I was feeling my age and paying attention to aging in ways I hadn't before. Certainly, there were the bodily aches and pains that reminded me that joints don't last forever, and I no longer ran into the ocean or day-dreamed of long backpacking trips. My feet and hips, in particular, were wearing out like an old rope pull.

But most of the ways that I was beginning to feel my age were more psychic than physical. A sense of urgency fueled me to set my sight on the work of making the world better for those on the edge. Before coming to the scrappy little church on 82nd Avenue, I had not yet found what I always called the Church of the Magnificat, that is, a church dedicated to reversing the fortunes of the rich and poor. In my choices, if not in my aspirations, I had repeatedly chosen a traditional path of career and comfort. Feeling my age meant realizing not only that there's no time like the present, but the present is, indeed, the only time.

"I want to be at a church that takes ministry with the poor seriously," I answered. "I think I've been looking for that my whole life."

"That we do," answered Mary. "We have no choice. It's who's around us. It's who we are."

That had been the most gratifying part of the interview. I didn't tell Mary that many churches existed among the poor and still managed to ignore them.

"Well," said Sharon at the end, stretching the syllable into two, "we're glad you want to come join us. We need to get a vote from the rest of the board."

I realized then that they would be a tough bunch, but not because they were mean-spirited people. They had been beaten up spiritually over the years and didn't know why anyone would want to come there. It was mysterious to them that I would be willing to leave a church like the one I served in Seattle.

I was to begin work on April 1. If I had no first-hand knowledge, in those early weeks, of the wounds of individual congregation members, I did have a sense of the woundedness of the parish as a whole. The parish had struggled over the past several years in ways that many churches did. A beloved priest left five years earlier and after that several false starts had left them bereft of leadership, funding and people. The Episcopal Bishop in the area had given them some money and told them to hire me. I was their last, best hope.

I had some experience working with congregations in dire straits and everyone agreed that I was the right person to enter into this community's particular crossroads. Even without knowing that I'd come to the church a bit of a mess from my recent wrong turn, in calling me, the community had chosen the road less traveled. With the local Episcopal Church higher-ups, the little congregation had signed on to an uncertain scenario of what church consultants call "radical redevelopment." To say they had *embraced* this scenario would be to put it a little too positively. But the alternative, based on the community's bank balance and shrinking, aging member-ship, would be closure and the end of a sixty-year presence on the rough corner of 82nd Avenue and Pine Street on Portland's east side. This choice for redevelopment was both a courageous and a reluctant one for my little congregation. It meant that church would no longer look as it had always looked, and that none of us would know for sure what would come next.

The opportunity was to scatter seeds without knowing what would spring up, what would thrive, and what would wither. All with a group who either had gardens of their own or considered themselves well past gardening age.

My plan, starting in early 2020, was to meet all the neighbors, have cof-fee with local business owners, host local forums, and learn what weighed upon the hearts and minds of the neighborhood's non-churchgoers. In short, my work was to grow the church into something that had meaning and value beyond its walls.

I had done this before. I had a strategy and a plan, right down to the decoration of my new office and the agenda for a series of all-parish conver-sations I would host every Sunday in May and June. I'd bought the markers and the newsprint. I knew I had my work cut out for me, and I thought I knew what that work was.

Then, on March 23, one week before my official start date, the gover-nor of Oregon joined other governors in issuing a "Stay-at-Home Order." Public worship was considered particularly dangerous, and the Episcopal Bishop of Oregon ordered churches to be closed until further notice. My office walls were bare, my ten-point plan was shelved, and I was about to start leading a small, elderly, non-tech-savvy congregation, with whom I had never worshiped, into a new future that none of us could anticipate or imagine.

Nothing in my training as a priest, nor in my planning for this particular parish, prepared me for the 2020 pandemic, also known as Coronavirus, COVID-19, or simply "this crazy time in which we live."

"Our physicality is one of the ways we are Good News in the world," I said to the camera, seeking out the viewfinder while wondering what "physicality" means when you cannot hug or shake hands or share a meal with a community for whom those things have always been considered essential.

I had abundant experience with trying things, failing, and trying something new. My recent decision to leave Seattle was just one example. But I was noticing that a feature of pandemic life for many people was adaptation. Like a species under stress, those who would not just survive COVID-19, but also thrive, might be people who were skilled at trying new things.

In June 2020 I had a conversation with Neil and Tina, a neighborhood couple adjusting to what we then were still calling "lockdown." Tina had long worked from home as a website developer and the pandemic did not affect her work the way it affected her husband: he was a guitar teacher.

"I've been teaching on Zoom occasionally for a while," Neil said, sipping on a glass of wine on the other side of my computer screen. "But doing it all the time is different. It's 'agility testing' for teaching and communication. Right now, it's a positive challenge."

I was encouraged by this description of life on Zoom as an agility test and as a positive challenge. I wasn't sure it could be that way for me; I found it exhausting, perhaps because I traded in open-ended interaction rather than transfer of knowledge. But Neil's energy made me hopeful.

"The Jazz Festival is another challenge altogether," said Tina from her screen in another room of the same warm-lit house.

"Tell me about the Jazz Festival," I asked. I'd come to a church where "the arts" meant the Seattle Opera and Pacific Northwest Ballet. I loved knowing that my former congregation loved these things, but a neighborhood jazz festival was much more my speed. My heart warmed with Neil's description of a grassroots music collective that had formed and grown over the past three years, with a weeklong event each August.

"Not this year, of course," he said. "We're trying to figure out how to do something this year that will support local artists and get something to people. Stay tuned." I looked forward to hearing more.

In my church neighborhood I watched as local businesses set up on-line retail overnight, or learned to teach guitar through a computer screen, or offered socially distanced personal training in a nearby park. I didn't yet know what it would look like, but I knew I was going to need to learn to pivot.

The dozen or so parishioners who gathered on-line were a rag-tag bunch. Preaching into a smartphone camera in an empty church was not the only way I'd tried to lead worship. For the first few weeks, the little community gathered for readings, prayers, songs, and a brief sermon on the ubiquitous Zoom video conferencing platform. Most of my parishioners were people I had never met in the flesh, and I was seeing them each week as little squares on a grid across my computer screen. Some were in their pajamas, and some ate breakfast while we watched the worship video together. One woman held the phone to her ear throughout, not realizing the phone's camera gave the rest of us a close-up view of the side of her head and the advancing scary darkness of her outer ear.

My Seattle congregation boasted three Sunday services in a beautiful building, a recently-restored mid-century modern gem decorated in forest colors with a steeply pitched roof topped with skylights on which birds often perched, scratching on the glass and drawing worshippers' attention upward.

Saints Peter & Paul, by contrast, was a humbler place, built earlier in the 20th century when its neighborhood was even farther away from the center of the city. Like a lot of churches, the building was noisy: built from Oregon timbers, it creaked with every breeze and sometimes I could hear its old bones settling noisily with no prompting from wind or rain. The interior had a shabby feel, with its beat-up floor, dust on window-ledges, and uneven lighting. The décor was what I affectionately call "Anglo-Catholic kitsch": doll-like statues of patrons Peter and Paul perched on wall-mounted pedestals on either side of the altar, multiple Marys from different eras and styles around the space, including two offerings of Our Lady of Guadalupe, one a heavily shellacked poster on plywood, and the other an intricately woven and beaded tapestry made in Mexico by a relative of a member of the Latino congregation.

The Guadalupe tapestry was rimmed in white Christmas lights. The first time I saw this I smiled to myself, remembering a conversation in Seattle in which I suggested that we use those same little white string lights to brighten up the half-dozen large live fir trees that decorated the altar area every Christmas, creating the effect of a dark forest. My suggestion was met by surprise bordering on horror. And here were those same string lights on display all year round! This added to the eclectic nature of the worship space; no striving for consistency or perfection there. Early on I knew I would need to shed some of my bias, instilled during my priestly training, for everything to be done "decently and in good order," as St Paul admonished.

I longed to gather with my little congregation in person and gradually accepted that it was not going to happen for a long time. Although most of my social and work life had moved, over a short amount of time, from face-to-face interactions to meetings and other so-called gatherings on Zoom, the two-dimensionality of on-line life intensified the longing to be in the same room with the people of my new parish. In the beginning of the pandemic, people used Zoom for meetings, happy hours, family reunions, exercise classes, dance parties, and costume contests. By mid-May 2020, the thrill of all that had worn off and everyone was "done" with Zoom, wanting to use it only for essential meetings.

Most people I knew found Zoom exhausting, in spite of the joys of working from home in pajama bottoms. A social worker I know explained one reason Zoom is so tiring: a concept called "objective social awareness," defined as "attention focused on the self as a socially evaluable object." Apparently, when you are looking at yourself while others are also looking at you, as one does, inevitably, on the Zoom screen, it is impossible not to evaluate yourself in a way that you don't at home in the bathroom mirror. In other words, according to some social psychology experts, when we're looking at ourselves while someone else is looking at us, we are engaged in evaluative—judging—behavior. We are evaluating ourselves while thinking about how someone else might be judging us at the same time. The Zoom experience becomes more performative than interactive, something comfortable for performers (and perhaps explains why so many introverts take to the stage) and tiring for the rest of us.[1]

The other reason Zoom is exhausting is that no matter how many videos we watch on how to position ourselves, our lighting, and our computers, if Zoom is the next best thing to being there, it's a far distant second. I still felt the absence of body language—in fact, I'd heard from colleagues that we're actually supposed to withhold facial reactions. More experienced

---

1. Jian, Manyu, "The reason Zoom calls drain your energy," BBC, April 22, 2020, https://www.bbc.com/worklife/article/20200421-why-zoom-video-chats-are-so-exhausting

Zoom-users call this "protecting the face." Eye contact can be fabricated by looking directly at the little laser-green camera light; when you really look at someone's eyes, their perception is that you're looking elsewhere. Having access only to shoulders-up cues and the lack of eye-contact forces us to hang on someone's every word without accompanying non-verbal information.[2] This lack of true connection was as exhausting to me as the unconscious self-judging that happened whenever I saw myself on-screen.

Those first weeks I sat at my desk at home, preaching from notes I'd taped to the side of my screen. Sometimes they'd fall down. Sometimes I'd pick them up; sometimes I'd wing it. My desk sits along a wall of windows looking out onto four house-sized maple trees, which, in April, were starting to bud. It was strange to preach sitting at my desk like that; stranger still to feel the tug of early spring days while I sat there, clergy shirt and collar on top, yoga pants and bedroom slippers underneath. I felt like a fraud, speaking my so-called priestly wisdom into the green LED at the top of my screen, pretending I was making eye contact.

After a few weeks of "Zoom Church," I wanted to try live streaming the service in the empty church. I asked the singers and piano player to move into the pews so I could preach to someone besides my phone held in Mark's hands like a second mask over his eyes. The others, all three of them, sat spread out in the sunny church, its emptiness overshadowing all its other good qualities.

"Imagine if we were to inhabit our bodies with the same sense of wonder and surprise that the first disciples have when they realize that Jesus is truly there in the flesh," I said into the camera.

When I watched that first sermon in the church, I saw a middle-aged woman whose grey hair, desperately in need of a trim, hung over her face, a blurred fur hat in June. The hairline was not the only thing that was blurry. I wanted to move around in the space, to inject my own energy into the place that had been paralyzed for some time. The result, though, was a fuzzy ineffective presence in a space booming with vacancy.

I was going to need to try something else. Which was, as I was learning, part of the coronavirus story, and had always been my own story, pandemic or no pandemic.

---

2. Julia Sklar, "'Zoom Fatigue' is taxing the brain. Here's why that happens," April 24, 2020, https://www.nationalgeographic.com/science/2020/04/coronavirus-zoom-fatigue-is-taxing-the-brain-here-is-why-that-happens/?utm_source=pocket&utm_medium=email&utm_campaign=pockethits

Chapter 2

Running Water

A t the start of the pandemic, churches everywhere drained their baptismal fonts and emptied out their holy water stoups. If you're like me and you always wondered, "stoup" is the medieval name for the little dish many churches have mounted in a doorframe near the entrance filled with holy water—usually water that has been blessed in baptism—that people use to cross themselves as they go in and out of church. It's often shaped like a scallop shell, sometimes made of brass, sometimes stone. The dry, empty stoup at Saints Peter & Paul was a constant reminder of the emptiness of the church. My habitual reach for it with my fingers every time I walked through the interior arches into the worship space the first few weeks was a regular reminder that things were not quite right. My own feelings of dryness in the early days of the pandemic matched the stoup, with its jagged white circle around the edge left over from the evaporated water. We knew there would not be holy water for a while, at least not in the traditional sense. It was all part of figuring out what it meant to be the Church in a time when gathering was not possible.

During the early months of the pandemic, the governing body of Episcopal churches in Oregon made funds available for churches to use in order to see them through what we all thought would be a short crisis. Many churches used these emergency funds for recording equipment or software or other supports for making online worship meaningful and even captivating.

The thought of any of that overwhelmed me. I had figured out early on that I hated online church. I could not imagine any technology that would make it better.

"It sounds like everything is falling apart and we're scrambling to keep the church relevant," I said to Megan, my tall priest friend with whom I often shared eyerolls, figurative and otherwise, about the church. "What if it's not? What if online church, no matter the bells and whistles, is not what people need right now?"

"We still need to stay connected, though, right?" We were out for a walk and Megan's legs were longer than mine. I jogged a couple steps to catch up so I wouldn't feel like her words were coming back to me over her shoulder.

"Yes, and we need to reassure people, too. But some days I don't feel like the best person to do the reassuring." I'd been a priest fifteen years longer than Megan and always hated to let on that I didn't know everything. "Or even if I can find wise words of comfort, do I need fancy video-editing software to get my point across?"

We went on like this for a while. It felt like an impossible situation. The Zoom fatigue I'd begun to experience in the earliest days of the pandemic had not gotten better. I wasn't interested in supporting this disembodying experience, especially not when we were surrounded by so much suffering.

"What I really wonder about is whether we can use the funds to help people outside the church." This was not always a strong suit for churches. I asked Anneliese, then director of Rahab's Sisters, a ministry of hospitality at Saints Peter & Paul, what the greatest need was among the guests she saw every Friday night.

"Running water. No contest." She paused for a moment to blow her bangs out of her eyes. "Everyone talks about handwashing, but our people have no way to wash their hands. And all the restrooms in parks are closed."

When the pandemic became headline news in early 2020, running water was a constant theme. Months before we were all told to wear masks and work from home, every bit of news included reminders to wash our hands, front and back, for twenty seconds. Celebrities washed their hands on the news. Opera singers demonstrated washing hands in the time it took to sing "Happy Birthday." *Pray the Lord's Prayer slowly, like you mean it*, said one Bishop to his flock on YouTube. I was not the only one whose hands were red and sore all the time. My coat pockets bulked up with small tubes of lotion alongside hand sanitizer as my constant companions.

In addition to hand sanitizer and lotion in every pocket of every coat in my closet, I stocked alcohol wipes. (We all had our favorite supplies, right?) I used them to clean my phone and occasional doorknobs. On another one of my walks with Megan early on in the pandemic, I stopped to take a photo of a violet pushing its way through a sidewalk crack. I reached into a pocket for my phone and out fell an individually wrapped alcohol wipe. It landed inches from the violet.

Megan gave one of her big laughs.

"You should take a photo of *that!*" she said.

After a long exchange of emails and phone calls with representatives from the City of Portland, I was introduced to a private contractor who had designed a low-cost handwashing station that was easy to manufacture, deliver, and maintain. It was hard for me to visualize it when he described it over the phone, but when I saw it nestled in the half-fenced smoking area of the church parking lot, I was in love. The design was a sixty-five-gallon drum with another, slightly smaller drum inside it; the interior drum held clean water; the exterior drum collected wastewater. A foot pedal at the bottom pumped water into a built-in enamel sink built into the top, with a hand-pumped soap dispenser attached.

After a while it became part of the landscape. Over the months of spring turning into summer, it got a little dinged up like much of the church building. We paid the people who sold it to us to come out weekly to empty the dirty water, refill the clean water, restock the soap, and occasionally replace the soap dispenser that regularly broke.

In the hottest days of 2020 the handwashing station in its corner of the parking lot, often surrounded by trash, was a little oasis where people could come and run water over their hands. Once, when I pulled into the parking lot, I watched as a skinny guy took off his weathered t-shirt and pumped the foot pedal until the water streamed out, soaked the shirt, and used it to spread cool water all over his head, neck and chest. He closed his eyes and washed his face, water dripping onto his oil-stained jeans. It was a small respite from the elements of living outdoors, but a respite nonetheless.

Water has been a locus for radical hospitality for a long time. Not only the Bible, but mythology through the centuries in both hemispheres is full of stories about water as respite and salvation.

Underneath an Orthodox church outside of the West Bank city of Nablus in what was once Samaria, and is now under the Palestinian Authority, is an ancient well. Legend has it that Jesus stopped there on a hot day while traveling from Galilee to Jerusalem. He introduced himself to a woman as "living water" and she famously believed him. Like centuries of women before and since, her job was to fetch water at the well. The encounter she had was bizarre: she meets a man midday which is itself unusual, and he tells her all about herself. He lays out her complicated marital history that would have been a source of shame in her community.

It is her community's well and so Jesus asks her for a drink; she complies as he sits in the hot noonday sun of the Judean desert. Jesus returns her hospitality by inviting her into the idea of living water, and she says yes. She opens herself to his interpretation of her life story—living in shame with one husband after another leaving her with a thirst slaked only by the water he promises, living with shame that is, like thirst, washed away by the generous encounter with a stranger in the midday sun. She comes away with a new self-understanding and tells all her friends.

This is a remarkable story because it is one of the few actual theological conversations that Jesus has in the gospel texts, that is, a conversation about what *God* is up to. Not only that, but Jesus has the conversation in a symbolically significant place with a symbolically significant person—a Samaritan who would have been considered an outcast in the religious tradition in which Jesus was raised. Not only that but she is a Samaritan *woman*, who would have been considered an outcast, well, everywhere. The result of the encounter is that a person outside of Jesus' own people is the first to fully receive an understanding of God as the source of life itself. On receiving that news, the first thing the woman does is invite others in.

Jesus and the woman he meets at the well trade hospitality. She gives him cool water; he gives her an invitation to belong in the new world he teaches about. She passes along the hospitality she receives to her neighbors.

I made my first visit to the Holy Land[1] in January 2017. It was a densely packed eleven days spent on a tour bus going from one pilgrimage site to the next. I had wanted to make the trip for a long time, and finally, with my son away at college and a generous scholarship from my bishop,

---

1. People of faith who visit the region indeed find it holy, as I have over the years that I have visited. However, I have long suspected that many of us call the area "The Holy Land" simply because it is easier to manage than "Israel" or "Israel-Palestine" or "Israel including the Occupied Territories" or any other appellation that is both true and fraught with controversy and struggle. Hundreds of books tell the story of the land and its centuries-old conflict. A few I can recommend are: *At the Entrance of the Garden of Eden*, by Yossi Klein Halevi (Harper Collins, 2002), *The Lemon Tree: An Arab, a Jew, and the Heart of the Middle East*, by Sandy Tolan (Bloomsbury, 2007), and *Jerusalem: the Biography*, by Simon Sebag Montefiore (Knopf, 2012).

the timing and the price were right. We arrived near midnight after a long flight from Seattle to San Francisco to Tel Aviv, followed by a two-hour bus ride eastward to our hotel, where half an Ambien helped me drop off to sleep despite hurtling through space and time zones for nearly twenty-four hours.

The next morning, I stepped into rubber travel slippers and stepped out my hotel room door onto a terracotta tile corridor open to the hotel's lush landscaping. I followed the path down some steps to a narrow gravel beach and slipped off my shoes. Lapping at my toes was the Sea of Galilee, also known as the Sea of Tiberias, also known as the lake of Gennesaret. Our retreat center was one of several pilgrim lodges along the shores of Galilee where later that day we would visit, in rapid succession, a slew of sites where significant stories in the life of Jesus were thought to have taken place. The Sea of Galilee is a wide spot in the Jordan River that flows the length of Israel, from the Lebanese border to the Dead Sea.

Later in the week our group would visit the muddy bank of the Jordan River where Jesus is thought to have been baptized—a significant site for pilgrims everywhere. For me, though, that moment of dipping my toes into the sea of Galilee was the moment that most strongly evoked my own baptism.

Jacob's well, where Jesus met the woman of Samaria, draws water that seeps from the water table under land that has been fraught with territorial violence since the days of Rahab through today. Down some narrow stone stairs one can find the original well. An attendant lowers the bucket upon request and brings up cold clear water for us to dip our fingers into.

The church is home to an Orthodox priest who fits the part with a beard down to his waist and a black zucchetto covering his bald head in the dim light of the church gift shop where he works. When I visited there with a group of pilgrims, he was filling small vials with water from the well, sealing them with brown wax, and selling them for ten shekels apiece, or about two dollars and fifty cents. I bought one and found, when I got home, that the seal had broken, and the water had leaked out all over the socks I'd wrapped it in. There was something holy and right about these drops of water from an ancient, storied well serving as prewash for my travel laundry.

Baptism was not something I'd thought much about, even after I began attending church as a young adult in the early eighties. Baptism was something I'd seen in the movies, like Robert Duvall's character in *Tender Mercies*, or Michael Corleone's infant in *The Godfather*.

But one Sunday in November 1983, as we drove home from church back across the Charles River to Cambridge in his orange Volkswagen Beetle, my friend Thom asked me if I'd ever been baptized. The thought had never occurred to me. Thom was someone I'd met in rooms where people help each other stay sober, and he was one of the wise ones whom I looked to for advice from time to time. He was also the person who introduced me to the Episcopal Church a few months before this particular Sunday.

"I doubt it. My dad would never have allowed it. He was always explaining how one could be Jewish and atheist at the same time. My mother was christened as a Unitarian, but she never attended church."

"You should talk to Al about it."

Al Kershaw was the priest at the church. He was famous for the crushing bear hugs he gave during the exchange of the Peace, and I'd been the beneficiary of several such hugs in the months I'd been attending church. Getting a hug from Al, who didn't know my name or anything about me, was one of the unspoken benefits of sitting in the second pew.

"Really? It's not too late?"

"Too late for what?"

We had crossed the river and were now passing MIT, heading north toward my studio apartment.

"Too late to be baptized? I'm not exactly an infant in a long frilly christening gown."

Thom chuckled in this way he had, amused by this mix of hopelessness and naiveté. He looked straight ahead as he drove, thick tortoise-shell rimmed glasses between his eyes and the windshield. I fumbled absentmindedly in my bag and my hands shook a bit. I was excited.

"It's never too late," said Thom as we turned off Massachusetts Avenue onto my street. "I bet priests especially love baptizing adults; it's like bringing a new sheep into the fold. You should call Al."

I'd never called a priest. As we sat in his car in front of my building, Thom explained that other people did, all the time, and that Al would be happy to meet with me and talk about baptism or anything else. The VW idled like a motorcycle; Thom kept a hand on the stick shift knob to keep it from shaking.

"Really," he said again. "Call him. I bet you anything he'll be happy to talk with you."

A few weeks later, Al came down from his office in the tower of the church building to meet me at the church's street door. We rode the ancient elevator up to his office. The elevator was barely larger than a phone booth, painted black with a grate for a ceiling. Through the grate I watched the cables alternately shorten and slacken as we moved slowly and noisily upward. There was hardly room for two of us. I wondered whether Al made multiple trips when counseling a couple or whether he sent them up ahead.

He smelled like shaving cream and eucalyptus, with a laugh so loud the little old ladies in church kept their distance. Before becoming a priest, he'd been a football player and then a jazz musician. His office walls were covered with art, framed photos of him with babies and bridal couples, snatches of poetry, and bookcases. I thought he was God, whatever God was.

"Tell me about yourself," he said in his big booming voice and his southern accent.

I'd never talked with a priest before but telling him about myself was surprisingly easy.

"I was kind of a mess when I was younger. Maybe I still am." I fiddled with a rubber band in the pocket of my denim jacket. "I guess I always feel like I'm in between hard things."

I told him a bit about my youthful experience of failure, despair, and longing. I told him how I used to call it "drinking to excess," avoiding, as people do, the A-word. *Alcoholism.* This was a disease of faith from which I suffered acutely for less than ten years, but long enough for me to sit up and take notice. It was a cancer of the soul. When I drank, I drank until I puked. I was usually so sick the next day that I could not read or work or think, and the only thing that helped was smoking weed or drinking more beer. The cancer of the soul said: *You are weak, you don't matter, and you feel like shit because you are shit.* It was like the good angel and the bad angel except that when the alcoholism became one with the soul, there was no longer any good angel on the shoulder, only the bad angel. The bad angel said: *go ahead, sleep with that guy; you don't deserve any better. Go ahead, steal that cash, stick that steak up your shirt and cook it for breakfast with the guy whose name you can't remember, still asleep in your apartment. Write that bad check. Tell that lie.* The drinking was me searching for faith and dousing it at the same time.

By the time I sat in Al's office talking about baptism, I had learned not to drink, one day at a time. The bad angel was still there on my shoulder, but now had a formidable opponent.

I told Al about visiting Amherst the previous summer for the first time since my half-drunken, half-frightened departure from UMass. I stayed a week in an old friend's house, spending days at the Amherst College library, trying to turn my senior thesis on Chaucer into a scholarly article. I stared through heavy plate-glass windows at a campus I never attended, remembering the mess of my two years at the university up the street three years earlier. I told Al about a morning run during that summer week, along the orchard ridge, where the blossoms were long gone from the trees, but I could smell the promise of apples to come. As my feet crunched the roadside gravel, all the dangers and despair of my adolescence flashed across my view like an old horror movie.

"Suddenly, I realized I had barely escaped with my life," I said in Al's office, tucking a foot under myself on the dark green leather couch. "Something, someone saved me. From myself, I think."

Al was silent for a moment, his fat fingers splayed out from each other, hands together at the fingertips. "Thank God," he said in his deep Kentucky voice. And again, "Thank God."

"I just cry all through church every Sunday."

"Of course you do," Al said. "Resurrection is a hard and scary thing, and don't ever let anyone tell you different."

He talked about sin. As he did so, he moved his legs—one at a time or together—on and off a small square ottoman in front of his well-worn wing chair. "My old knees don't like sitting still," he explained.

Al defined sin as *alienation*, being separated from God, sometimes through very little fault of our own. "When we're separated from God—which, sad to say, we all are, much of the time," he said as he switched legs, "when we're separated from God, we do things we don't want to do."

I thought sin was all the bad things I'd done: stealing money from my mother's purse, taking rolls of toilet paper from public restrooms, or sleeping with a friend's boyfriend. Certainly, these were things I didn't want to do, but at the time, I thought I had to. Would it be different if I weren't so alienated from God?

Al said baptism meant saying "yes." Yes to Jesus, yes to my own life story, yes to being part of a community of faith, yes to the possibility of resurrection.

I got most of this, except for one thing. Jesus. Jesus made me squirm in my chair and clench my teeth. I never thought of Jesus other than as a figure in a painting, bloody on the cross, or as a giant statue, arms wide in invitation, but frozen in marble just the same. I was willing to overlook my discomfort with Jesus, so I could get all the other stuff Al talked about: grace, community, and resurrection. If I was going to enter the waters of all that baptism promised, Jesus would need to be there, too. I wanted to say yes.

I was baptized in April 1984. It was the Saturday before Easter, Holy Saturday, and the service was Emanuel Church's version of the Great Vigil of Easter.

Another adult was being baptized at the same time; a thin pale guy in tortoise-shell glasses named Michael. I pondered what his story might be. Maybe he had sat in the back, anonymous in that church where so many came late and left early. Maybe he met with Al, who would have told him—as he had told me—about gaining a whole new family through a few drops of water. I still didn't see how that was going to happen. Maybe behind his mousy looks he was one of God's chosen people, hand-picked to lead the revolution, while I stood judging him.

The church administrator, Sandra, was there: a round woman in thick glasses. Every Sunday in church the person who read prayers said, "Please continue to pray for the repose of the soul of Mildred Z., and for her daughter Sandra in her grief." We prayed the same prayer for over a year, and I felt like I knew them both, mother and daughter so close that death hadn't divided them. That weekly prayer for Mildred made me consider, for the first time, that the fissure between this life and whatever happened next was not a stone cliff or a planetary divide but was instead a thin filament, a porous membrane.

Also gathered in front of the altar were a handful of women who had spent Holy Saturday giving the building its annual spring cleaning. I recognized their faces, church ladies who lived behind the scenes. I'd never been there when the church was so dark and silent. The traffic noise from Newbury Street was the only way I knew it was Saturday afternoon rather than some mysterious moment taking place outside of time.

We circled a small table where Al had placed some linen and a small cruet of water. A large candle stood next to the table, taller than I was and decorated with Greek letters. Al lit the wick from a flint and then prayed about the lighting of the candle, a prayer so long I wondered if it would ever end. The lighting of the candle marked the end of Lent and the coming of Easter. The light from the candle glinted off the cruet of water.

The people around me took turns reading the lessons about the story of creation, the parting of the Red Sea, the valley of dry bones. I knew the story of creation from reading *Paradise Lost*, but the others were new to me. The story of the Red Sea went on forever. Over and over again, all of Pharaoh's horses, chariots, and chariot drivers went into the sea.

The waters of the Red Sea were waters of liberation. But I was impatient for all those long readings and unfamiliar prayers to be over so we could get to the baptism.

It was years later that I learned that the Exodus story was the foundational story of the people of Israel, people who wandered in the desert for forty years after that miraculous crossing. I would later visit that desert, the dry rocky ground between the northern shore of the Red Sea separating Egypt from modern-day Jordan, and the land flowing with milk and honey.

I can see why all that wandering happened. The scenery is intoxicatingly beautiful, nourishing to the eye, but rarely to the body. The story has it that Moses and the people climbed up to the top of Mount Nebo, where they looked west to the promised land. If the view from Mt. Nebo were not always shrouded in haze rising from the Red Sea, one would be able to see the city of Jericho where Joshua, successor to Moses, sent spies to investigate the city. Those were the spies who encountered the hospitality of Rahab at the edge of the city as part of their first experience of the land of promise.

As I learned more about the story over years, and as I visited the desert where the Israelites wandered, I still remembered listening to that story in that circle of people in the fading light of the afternoon before Easter all those years before.

Finally, Michael and I stepped into the center of the small circle of worshippers. Al asked the six questions we'd talked about in meetings to prepare for this afternoon. Still, I felt unprepared.

"Do you renounce Satan and all the spiritual forces of wickedness that rebel against God?"

Satan? The forces of wickedness? This sounded like Dark Shadows or Star Trek. But who was I *not* to renounce the forces of wickedness? So, I responded, "I renounce them."

"Do you renounce the evil powers of this world, which corrupt and destroy the creatures of God?"

Sure. Just like Superman.

"I renounce them," we said. Al had told each of us the importance of saying "I" even though there were two of us answering the questions.

"Do you renounce all sinful desires that draw you from the love of God?"

This one was easier. *Say yes. Turn toward the light.*

"I renounce them," we each said. Michael's voice was even shakier than mine.

"Do you turn to Jesus Christ and accept him as your Savior?"

The my-savior language made me itch. I didn't think of Jesus this way. "I do."

"Do you put your whole trust in his grace and love?"

Why not? Better him than the goats I'd been falling in love with my whole life.

"I do."

"Do you promise to follow and obey him as your Lord?"

Just like an old-time wedding. *Really? Jesus?*

"I do."

Al prayed a long prayer over the tiny cruet of water:

> We thank you, Almighty God, for the gift of water.
> Over it the Holy Spirit moved in the beginning of creation.
> Through it you led the children of Israel out of their bondage
> in Egypt into the land of promise. In it your Son Jesus
> received the baptism of John . . . .

Another jumble of words and images. I looked around the circle. Sandra had her eyes closed, nodding ever so slightly to the cadence of the words, familiar to her. Thom, who was taking me out for a celebratory dinner afterwards, looked at his shoes. I liked how everything needed to be blessed: the candle, the water, the people.

With his thumb, Al made the sign of the cross on my forehead with water from the cruet, speaking words I knew he'd said hundreds of times before: *I baptize you in the name of the Father*—as his thumb slid down my brow from the part in my hair to just above my eyes—*and of the Son*—as his thumb moved horizontally across my forehead—*and of the Holy Spirit.* He ended with his large hand on the top of my head, its weight grounding me. I learned that the Greek for "in the name of" is "into the name"; I was indeed joining a new community.

And that was neither the beginning nor the end of my deliverance like so many Hebrew slaves from Egypt. I only knew that the word was *Yes*.

When I was in East London years later, my mentor-priest Father Brian told me about meeting a sex worker on a crowded street who asked him to baptize her. He bought a bottle of water at the nearest mini-mart and poured it over her head as she knelt in a nearby alley. In neither my case, nor hers, was the experience like Robert Duvall in *Tender Mercies*. No tub, no splashing, no dunking. No wading into the muddy River Jordan in a white robe with a choir singing "Wade in the Water" behind me. No huge cathedral service. But I felt the water, including the drops that dribbled down my nose, and I felt the sign of the cross, Al's thumb firm and cool, pressing hard on my forehead.

Thirty-six years later, now a priest feeling my way through the early days of a pandemic, there was no celebration of the Easter Vigil, the long, mystical service of readings and promises. I'd mailed home to each parishioner a booklet with some prayers for that Saturday, as well as instructions to light a candle and to sprinkle oneself with water at a certain point in the prayers as a reminder of our baptism. Easter Vigil at home alone felt empty and strange, even more than amid that small circle at Emmanuel Church in Boston so long ago.

Chapter 3

Shaping a Priest

Th here is a scene in the 1991 movie *The Commitments* where the main character interviews prospective members of a new band. As each person comes to his door, he asks the question: "Who are your influences?" He judges the musicians on their split-second response.

In my first few months at my new parish, I was thinking about the influencers in my life and wondered who had helped to shape the movers and shakers of my new congregation. I asked some of the older women to tell me about who their influences had been over the years. We were on Zoom; I'd sent an email saying I'd love to learn more parish history, particularly about the priests who had formed them. *I'm always up for a trip down memory lane*, one woman had written back. There were five of us on the screen: Linda, Pauline, Sharon, Jeannie, and myself. Each of the women had been in the congregation for decades: Jeannie was born into the parish in 1960, Pauline came around that same time, Linda moved into the neighborhood and started attending in 1980, and Sharon was the newcomer who arrived in 1990.

Pauline began: "Father H. was the priest when I came. My family was having a tough time and he saved us. He made us feel so at home, he really took me in."

Pauline was in her seventies, with a demeanor that could most easily be described as "spry." She was recently widowed and had told me she experienced a lot of loneliness. She also spent a lot of time walking with friends and even traveling during the pandemic. She was petite and blond, and always answered the question *How are you?* by saying she was keeping busy. I had never seen her so animated as when she talked about Father H.

"It wasn't just my family. Everybody loved him. He really built this church up." Her blue eyes sparkled. "He started a boys' choir, and in the summertime he invited all the boys to a church summer camp. He called it his 'boys' ranch.'" She leaned into the camera. "Everybody loved the boys' choir and the boys' ranch. Come to think of it, you might say he was really a boys' priest."

All of this gave me pause. I was surprised that Pauline spoke of this "boys' priest" and his summer camp without explanation or caveat, given the many distressing stories in the news for the past generation about men who had been emotionally scarred for life by sexually inappropriate priests. But people who knew Father H. spoke of him with reverence and respect.

"Father S. was here when I came," said Sharon, moving thick dark bangs off her forehead as she talked. "His main influence was making you feel special when he told you that you were the best person to do something. Like, 'Sharon, you should be treasurer.' I ended up being treasurer for about nine years after that."

I heard other things about Father S. that earned him a place in the ladies' memory as a patriarch and an influencer: he saw the parish through what was, for many, the trauma of accepting women's ordination, a challenge for traditional parishes like Saints Peter & Paul in the late 1970s and early 1980s. He helped the congregation begin a community meal that was open to the public and that continues to this day.

"But he was single," Linda said. "It makes a difference, whether a priest has a family or not. We had more kids in the parish when we had Father H, or later when Father K was priest. They had kids and so other kids came. Of course, now . . . all the kids are grown, and we haven't had new ones for a long time."

My responses to the question of influencers would win *The Commitments* test for the quick answer award: Ed McIntyre, Ken Leech, and my father. Ed McIntyre was a priest at the small parish I discovered soon after moving to Portland in 1986, a crucial time in my own discovery of whether—and how—I might become a priest myself. Ken Leech first introduced me to the idea of a "public priest," whose parish, in his case, spanned continents. My father, a Jewish-Marxist-atheist, was the person in my family who got me.

Though my father remains my earliest and perhaps most enduring influence from child and young adulthood, my mother's influence was formidable. Hers was the impact I spent much of adolescence trying to escape. Her family was dominated by women who managed to be both powerful and needy, both successful in their chosen field and extremely neurotic. The chosen field was most commonly child-rearing; those who did not have children became painters, poets, or philanthropists, but were generally a nutty lot. My mother did everything well. She raised two children on delicious home-made bread, taught herself to paint, became an architect, designed and sewed costumes for several community theatre companies, built stage sets, and rebuilt several beautiful homes. She continues to explore the layers of her own life with curiosity and hope.

My best friend from college said once that no one could really know me until they visited me at Manchester-by-the-Sea, the summer home of the matriarchy. She meant, more precisely, the seventy coastal acres north of Boston that six generations called "Manch." It wasn't one thing about Manch that made her say that, it was everything: the sea and the view, the giant dining room table, my grandmother and her sisters for whom we dressed for dinner, the old dusty privilege of the house with its long-repurposed servants' quarters, the waves swirling and bursting against the rocks, the tide-pool treasure trove of sea stars and sand crabs . . . all of it was as much a part of me as the sooty streets in New York where my childhood friends and I roamed, looking for trouble.

Perhaps I was born with the genes to absorb the place, or perhaps the place seeped into me, summer after summer beginning when I was only a month old. In that place, the sound of the waves was the last thing I heard at night before falling asleep and the first thing I heard in the morning, even before waking up. The waves were my heartbeat.

The ocean was my family's God and their church: it was the place where we worshiped, and the object and source of our devotion. Not just any ocean, but the particular stretch of the Atlantic we could see from Manch. It was truly, as the famous protestant theologian Paul Tillich wrote, "the ground of our being." Our family's only weekly religious ritual outside the world of Manch was to drive generations of Irish maids, with names like Teresa, Bridie, and—of course—Mary, into downtown Manchester for Catholic mass, every Friday, Sunday, and Wednesday. I'd peeked inside Mary's Catholic Church and loved the red velvet hush of it; the smell of old wood.

When I was a child, I wished I had been named Isabella, mostly because of the Isabella Spoon. If I'd been Isabella, I would one day inherit the Isabella Spoon, a large, silver utensil, with a jeweled handle and a long history. No one ever actually used it; the spoon lived in a long brown flannel bag held closed with a silky brown drawstring. Every once in a while, my grandmother would take it out to show me.

"This is going to your Aunt Bella when I'm ready to part with it," she said one time. "But I'm not ready yet."

My seven-year-old self vowed then and there to name my daughter Isabella. The spoon had been passed from Isabella to Isabella for hundreds of years. Someone who had the spoon would certainly have a sense of her place in the world. She would know to whom she belonged. Maybe she would sparkle and shine, and everyone would want her the way I wanted that spoon. I used to think the spoon came from the Queen Isabella we learned about in school, the one married to Ferdinand, who sent Columbus to discover America in the Nina, the Pinta, and the Santa Maria.

"She was Spanish. *Our* original Isabella was English. No relation," my grandmother explained to me in her throaty smoker's voice.

Her piercing blue eyes matched my great-grandmother's, looking out at me from a family portrait in the dining room. My great-grandmother kept a diary and wrote in it almost every morning all her married life. Some days she wrote only a word or two. "Neuralgia. Drapes closed." "Dined downstairs today for the first time in weeks." On May 9, 1906, she wrote about my grandmother: "Third daughter born yesterday. Isabella, a homely child, but with a good appetite."

The sea would have been the first sound my grandmother ever heard. Her mother's eyes were the same color as the ocean, the first thing she ever saw. My grandmother inherited those sea-blue eyes and passed them on to my mother.

I did not inherit those perfect blue eyes, but rather my father's brown ones. From my mother and from her mother and grandmother before her, I inherited a certain perfectionism and quickness to judge. The distaste for judging others which I got from my father meant that I turned that judgmental tendency inward.

Sometimes, I wonder whether my mother married my father for his brown eyes, hoping for brown-eyed children as her way of stepping out of all that perfect blue. Years later, people who got to know each of my parents wondered what they ever saw in each other, because they were so different.

For my mother's part, it must have been the brown eyes, the dark Eastern European genes to stir the family pot.

My father had no interest in giving me one of the family names from the matriarchy: Isabella, Harriet, Margaret, or Elinor. Elinor was my mother's name, shortened to Nell. Sarah was my great-grandmother on my father's side. It was important for my father to claim for me that quintessential Hebrew name. He grew up hearing Russians hiss "Ssssaraahh" with scorn at Jewish women on buses and trains in Moscow. Everything bore a weight of meaning for my father. He dropped the "h" in Sarah because he wanted all of us to have four-letter names: Yura (the Russian version of George, which my father always preferred), Nell, Mark, Sara. Four people, four names, four letters.

Later we scattered in four directions. My parents divorced when I was ten, to no one's surprise. My mother remarried a year or two later and moved my brother and me from New York to Boston. My brother moved to China right after graduating from college and stayed there, except for the occasional business trip and an annual week at Manch. I moved from Boston to Portland in my mid-twenties.

Perhaps to rebel against the complicated system that was the matriarchal lineage in much of my family, I chose men as the people who helped to form me as a priest.

My circuitous and unlikely path to church and Jesus made sense to my father in a way that it didn't make sense to anyone else I was related to. The proper New England matriarchal family into which my father had married seemed to regularly wonder where I'd gone wrong. He watched my long journey to the priesthood become derailed in spots, first by a divorce from a man I never should have married, then by living in sin with Mark (yes, same name as my brother) whom I later married, and then by mothering the newborn Mark and I were fortunate enough to adopt. All of this made sense to my father, too.

My father liked to describe himself as a Wandering Jew. He was a restless soul from an early age. He was raised in Moscow and Berlin—part of his wandering narrative—by parents who were initially communist and then anti-communist. After a narrow escape from the Soviet Union, he immediately enlisted in the U.S. Army. After the war, he got his Ph.D. in Sociology from Harvard and spent the next five decades mining the great political thinkers of his day in search of a system that would help him to make sense of his life. In that process he mentored a generation of doctoral students in the importance of dialectic (a word I need to look up every time), and the value of wrestling with an idea or ideology from as many sides as possible. Whether he was arguing with the residents' association of his retirement community or the United States government, he never wavered in his critique of any system that created insiders and outsiders.

One weekend when I was in my mid-twenties, I visited my father in his Manhattan apartment. A dozen new books sat in a pile on his coffee table, and a brown shopping bag with a logo that read "The Dial Bookshop" held a half dozen more.

"I have something to tell you," he'd said, in the familiar way he had of preparing me for an important announcement.

I sat up a little straighter to let him know I was listening.

"I've become an anarchist," he said and waved his hands over the books. "These are a few books on anarchism. I'm really getting into it."

My father was a serial socialist, capitalist, anarchist, Buddhist, humanist. His was the atheist side of the family. Religion was foreign to him; searching for some kind of system of meaning was not. He took up ideologies like I took up crafts. I would buy a whole lot of supplies for, say, quilting, read up on the subject, and give up after a few weeks or a month. My father's ideology phases lasted longer than my crafty phases, but nothing was forever.

His announcement about becoming an anarchist stayed with me when I called him on the phone a year later and told him I was enrolling in Divinity School. I was twenty-six at the time. That year would turn out to be the opening act in a drama that continued for over a decade, between my first venture into theological study and returning to seminary in 2000.

"I think I might want to be a minister." I had to swallow hard. He was quiet on the other end for several beats. Was he wondering how the fruit had fallen so far from the Jewish-atheist tree? Was he thinking about the conservative evangelicals whose scandals appeared in the newspapers with some regularity?

"I think that's wonderful!" Another pause. "It suits you."

I hadn't realized how hard I was gripping the phone until I heard these words, and my fingers began to relax.

"You have a knack," he went on, "for putting things into words in ways that helps you connect with real people in a real way. Not intellectual, not bookish."

"I thought 'intellectual' was a good thing."

In my mother's side of the family, being able to quote classical English poetry from memory was always something to strive for and considered a sign of one's academic pedigree. Ivy League names were dropped into conversation with regularity, and nothing made my mother or grandmother beam more brightly than the prospect of one of their own graduating from Harvard, Yale, or Stanford.

"Nah. It's a curse. It gets in the way of being human."

Over the years I sent him drafts of sermons, letters to my local bishop asking to be ordained, and later seminary papers and more sermon drafts. He always engaged with the material the same way he would with his students, marking it up with a green felt-tip pen and usually telling me to both write shorter sentences and go deeper.

Ed McIntyre was my first priest-crush. When, in my heart, I tiptoed around the idea of vocation and wanting to be a priest, he was the priest I wanted to be like.

He was younger than the handful of priests I'd known before; when I met him he was thirty-two; I was twenty-seven. He wore jeans, played the guitar, and sang unselfconsciously. He seemed to carry on his shoulders a combination of lightness and heaviness: he never forgot the pain and struggle of the world but joked easily about his own foibles. I recall one day having lunch with him on a park bench near the church. He said a blessing over the food, asked God to help us to remember the hungry people around us in the city as well as the brokenness in the whole world. Then he opened a package of soy sauce to sprinkle over some California rolls and said: "Miso soup is the only proof I need of the existence of God."

The church where we met was in downtown Portland, and he often described himself as the chaplain to every houseless person in the city. Walking with him from the church to a nearby coffee shop or lunch spot was like walking through a big party. He knew everyone's names and stories and was always happy to see them. In a time when it was not uncommon to refer to houseless people as "bums" or "drunks," he treated people he met on the streets like relatives or neighbors.

I once asked Ed about his calling as we ate tomato soup at my dining room table.

"A lot of people will give you a lot of different answers to that question," he said with a chuckle and just a hint of an eyeroll.

"When I was thirteen, Jesus snatched me out of a life that was hell-bent," he went on, "so I thought I'd better do something for Him."

I could relate to the first part of what he said. When I started attending church after a life-threatening struggle with adolescent alcoholism, I had no trouble mapping Jesus' death-and-resurrection story onto my own, despite all of my other doubts and questions. But had I been "snatched"? And did I *owe* Jesus? And if I did, did I have anything to give back in return? I shared some of these musings with Ed as I refilled our water glasses.

"Do you think it's that important to be able to talk about a direct, personal experience of Jesus?" I asked.

"It certainly helps," he said, "although everyone is different."

I usually loved whatever Ed had to say, but I found this singularly unhelpful. Not only had I not had any kind of direct personal encounter with Jesus, I always had a hard time believing people who had. The ones who needed to talk about it all the time were kind of like vegans; they gave the rest of us who merely liked to eat plants and avoid factory-farmed animals a bad name.

Although I wasn't about to share any more of my inadequacy in the personal-encounter-with-Jesus department, I did say, "I always think I would have to, you know, get my act together in order to be a priest."

"Are you kidding?" he said. "It is when we are at our most broken that we are most Christ-like."

I loved listening to him say these words and yet at that time I could not imagine that the church would want me, or that I had anything to offer to the church other than my own enthusiasm, which, on bad days, felt more like a gaping longing. The change in my own sense of vocation and clarity about what it meant to be a priest, and what kind of priest I might be, turned out to be a long, and at times, indiscernible process.

Someone once described two different experiences of conversion: the Pop-Tarts variety, where something sweet, hot, and delicious emerges from a toaster, or the pickle variety, where a more nuanced and varied flavor emerges over time and immersion. In each case, the person's essence remains the same; in the case of Pop-Tarts, the experience of change is fast but temporary; in the case of pickles, the change is slow, sometimes dark, and always permanent. The evolution of my calling to the priesthood was like the evolution of cucumbers into pickles.

Ed left that downtown church a few years after we met to pastor a group of small and struggling congregations in an Episcopal mission to the

Native Dine people in the geographic area where the corners of Arizona, Utah, and New Mexico intersect. Ed had spent his life working with Native people. More than anyone else, he helped me understand what it meant to people whose spiritual and material identity was based in the land, to lose that land, to be displaced and their culture destroyed. But more than that, Ed modeled unswerving commitment to the poor, to anyone who had been pushed to the margins of society by those in power.

When I was ordained in 2003, he was the preacher. Ordination sermons traditionally ended with a "charge," when the preacher gives the person about to become a priest a word of commission or advice. Ed's charge to me was simple: "Remember that you are not to be a chaplain to the rich, but a bearer of good news to the poor." Little did I know at that time how difficult it would be for me to obey that charge.

Ed and I kept in touch intermittently over years. In the summer of 2018, I made a phone date with him; it would be our first actual conversation in years. His voice had the familiar lilting inflection of someone who had spent their whole life around native Americans on or near reservations. I'd driven through Seattle afternoon traffic to arrive early for a meeting so I could talk with him beforehand. I sat in my car, my journal resting on the steering wheel and earbuds in my ears so my hands could be free to take notes.

"Remember what you said when I was ordained, about bringing good news to the poor versus being a chaplain to the rich?" I asked him. "I'm failing at that, all the time."

I explained that my current congregation was made up of lovely people who wanted to care for the poor but always seemed to me to be deeply attached to the beauty of the physical space and the worship it held. My perception was that the attachment may have kept them from serving the poor in ways I felt all Christians were called to do. Perhaps I was failing, because I hadn't succeeded in helping the community to make more of an outward-facing shift. (This is when I reminded Ed what an impatient person I've always been.) I was feeling a tug to walk away from it all, to sell our beautiful condo with its Sunset magazine Seattle skyline-and-water view, return to our high-maintenance Portland house that felt like a favorite pair of slippers, and devote myself to building (or rebuilding) a church embedded in the grit and misery of the world. I explained that my dream would be to do "something meaningful" before I retired. I was fifty-nine at the time.

"First of all," he said, "as your friend, I would worry if you gave up on your dreams."

He paused. One of the things I appreciated about him was that he took his time to say what he wanted to say.

"If I were you, I would be in discernment. Because of all the corruption around us, the kind of discernment you're facing is not for the faint of heart. Most people in congregations are getting the faint-of-heart treatment from their priests."

In churchy circles, the word "discernment" has been about as overused as "lean in" over the past decade or two. The word literally means "to discover light," with "in the darkness" implied. But it gets used to make any kind of decision-making sound holy. *I need to discern what kind of car I'm going to get. I'm discerning whether or not to go to Florida for two weeks. I'm discerning whether so-and-so is a good therapist for me.* None of these are bad things. But the kind of discernment he spoke of seemed to be something different.

He went on to talk about the discernment I was doing as twofold: the personal discernment to pay attention to my dreams even if it meant disrupting my Seattle life, and the systemic discernment about whether *any* church is capable of the kind of ministry Jesus would recognize.

"Systemic evil shapes all of our consciousness," he said. "People sell their souls and don't even know it."

Years after he was my parish priest, I was still learning from him, and he was still making me ask myself hard questions. Had I sold my soul? Was it systemic evil that drew me to my Seattle church—with all its blessings— when my heart had for years longed to be at a place like Saints Peter & Paul? Might I have known better?

The pull to Seattle was a pull to a community who knew who they were and had no trouble asserting that truth, who offered heart-stirring and expertly orchestrated worship week after week, in a building that garnered national attention for its soaring roof and twenty-first-century sculpted altar and baptismal font.

It took being embedded in that community to learn that underneath the thoughtful, well-funded worship, and within that breathtaking building, lay a deep reluctance to engage with the world around them in the ways that I had learned from Ed, from my father, and from Ken Leech.

⊕

I first met Ken Leech when he gave a lecture in 1999 at Trinity Cathedral in Portland, nearly a year before I began seminary. Then in his early 60s, he had a rich accent from the North of England and bright blue eyes that occasionally had a little mischief in them, especially when talking about the foibles of British politicians and Church of England higher-ups. I fell in love with his accent and his wisdom. In his writings and on the North American church lecture circuit, Ken painted pictures of the East End of London as an ethnically diverse area with a history not only of extreme poverty and racial violence, but also of people working together to bring God into the world in ways that mattered. He called it "contextual theology."

Ken was the first speaker I'd ever heard who so eloquently linked, explicitly and implicitly, the inner life of prayer with the outer life of social justice, or "ministry in the world," as some called it. I wanted some of that.

Ken dressed in black t-shirts in summer and black turtlenecks in winter. He was extremely fond of the animated characters Wallace and Grommet, as well as Shaun the Sheep, and characters from these stories regularly populated his t-shirts, sometimes custom-designed by friends. He'd been a priest since the early 1960s, and I never saw him wearing a clerical collar. If he needed to dress like a priest, he simply donned a long black cassock to cover his t-shirt. He eschewed any trappings of church hierarchy. The only time he wore a clergy shirt and collar, he told me, was if he was asked to testify in court.

"I'd wear my birthday suit if it would help get someone out of jail!" he said once.

A large white handkerchief often overflowed out of his pants pocket, giving him a rumpled, almost disheveled look, although his words were thoroughly organized.

In the modern church, according to Ken, purity manifested itself in the tendency to press every linen to perfection, to polish silver until it shone with God's glory, and put both on the altar, calling it holy. This was the church I recognized, with its emphasis on beauty and order, which were a few of the things that had made it easy for me to latch onto the Episcopal Church. I recognized myself in the temptation to perfection, the pride I took in a beautifully set table, whether the table was my own dining table or the symbolic table that was part of Sunday worship.

Beauty and order, I heard Ken say in that first lecture of his at the cathedral, were all well and good if they didn't lead to exclusion and uniformity, which, unfortunately, they often did. I had been part of too many churches where there was one right way to sing the psalms, one proper form for bowing to the cross, kneeling, ringing bells, or setting up the altar for communion.

"Instead," he said, "we need mess, chaos, and disorder, in order to get on with the business of being human."

There he really had me. I also recognized myself in mess and chaos, and it was liberating, exhilarating, to hear someone talk about this, especially as I prepared to become a priest in the church in which he was steeped, and which he so deftly criticized.

Ken talked about a different kind of purity, the unadulterated calling to justice, and all the barriers to that kind of purity put up by organized religion. He reminded us that Jesus did not say "blessed are the peaceful," but rather "blessed are the peacemakers."

I was hooked.

When his talk ended, I joined the small crowd forming around Ken in the front of the room, people wanting to ask him a question or ask him to autograph their copies of his books. I had decided in a short time that he was no less than a gift from God. He offered a bigger and different way of being Christian and leading a parish than I had seen so far, except perhaps in Ed McIntyre. I held a copy of his book, *We Preach Christ Crucified*, but I was so star-struck that I didn't even think to ask him to inscribe it. As so often happened when faced with people I'd admired from afar, I felt shy. My palms were a little sweaty and I could feel myself blushing.

"Can I have your email address?" I asked hastily, handing him a pen and my book. He wrote it on the back page.

"I'm going to seminary," I said. "I want to come over there to the East End." *Gulp.* "Can I do an internship at your church?" I was glad that the crowd around us had thinned because my voice shook while I asked the question.

I blurted it out without much forethought, but I knew I wanted to immerse myself in the world that Ken talked about in his books and in his lectures. I knew that his was only a tiny slice of experience that I could find in many places, but something drew me to want to learn more about the church in London's East End. Ken talked about racial diversity, ministries to the poor that made a difference to people's lives, the people doing the work as well as the beneficiaries. For Ken, being a Christian naturally meant working for justice and economic equity, usually in the public arena. This was counter-cultural and sometimes subversive. I wanted to walk the streets of the East End which he spoke about; I wanted to be in the place where he advocated for justice and made space for people on the margins.

"We haven't taken interns for a long time," he answered, "but do write me and we'll figure something out." He blinked his eyes a couple of times in rapid succession the way some people do when they smile, making his face warm and inviting.

We kept in touch, and midway through seminary Ken contacted me and said he had found a priest who was willing to host our family for the summer, a priest who was involved in a program that helped prostituted women and girls. Something was beckoning me to the East End. It turned out that summer would change the course of my work in the church from that time forward.

Like my own family, and like a lot of churches in the mainline Protestant tradition, Saints Peter & Paul was a church that appeared, at first glance, to be dominated by women. Sometimes, as at my church, this was simply a matter of numbers. Even in its heyday, women at Saints Peter & Paul out-numbered men three to one. In 2020 the ratio was more like ten to one. And like my mother, grandmother, great-grandmother, and all the cousins and aunts who dressed for dinner with them over the decades, they revered men, although usually from a distance.

Like my church, the patron saints in my mother's family were men. Each generation was dominated by strong women whose stories filled each of several seaside houses, and each generation was devoted to their remote, solemn menfolk, who seemed to spend as little time at home as possible. There was Nathan Appleton, who made millions in the 1840s through the New England textile industry, success made possible by the abundance of cheap cotton grown by American slaves. There was Greeley Curtis, a Civil War general who fathered thirteen children, one of whom was my great-grandmother, Elinor. There was Charles Hopkinson, the painter who married her. As a wedding present, Greeley built the house with the huge ocean view, in which the couple raised five daughters, the middle one being my grandmother. That house was filled with Charles' paintings of his wife and daughters. He painted each of them as beautiful and strong, sometimes even stern and imposing.

In my family, the women brought to bear their personalities as vivid as their turn-of-the-century gowns and summer frocks. The men brought their various professions along with their sperm, but had little to say about day-to-day life there on the ocean, where the women always outlasted them. The reigning mothers would never have described themselves in language of power and control, nor viewed their menfolk as weak. And yet, looking back over the generations and my own decades of summers spent on the porch with the mothers and grandmothers, that was the case.

I was fascinated to explore how patterns of power and influence broke along gender lines at my church. A few weeks after the online meeting when I asked long-time members about their memories of priests who had influenced them, I gathered them again to ask about parish matriarchs.

Between the four women in squares on my screen they had spent sixteen decades at the church. Although in the email thread leading up to this gathering, they had shared dozens of names with me and with each other of women they remembered over the years, they were strangely silent when I asked my question:

"Who were the women who were 'a force' when you arrived at church?"

Finally, Pauline said: "There was Laurie, who ran the altar guild when I was young. What *was* her last name?"

Jeannie chimed in with the last name. Jeannie, who was younger than Pauline but had been born into the parish, seemed to know nearly everything.

"She had a glow about her," Pauline continued. All the women nodded; they all remembered her. "It was like an aura. She was so kind."

"She was short," added Jeannie, ever practical.

"And there was Jackie," said Linda, leaning into her computer with her soft voice and bad hearing. "She always had a hug for you."

"And birthday cards," said Sharon. "She gave out birthday cards to everyone even if she didn't know when your birthday was." She smiled with the memory of Jackie, now long gone.

"She even sent birthday cards to my sons!" said Linda. "And they hardly ever went to church. She had quite a list."

"Were there women in the past who seemed to have control over some aspect of church life?" I was again met with silence and blank stares.

"All the ladies were so welcoming to me when I came," said Sharon eventually. She was the newest arrival to the church. She had been coming since 1990.

I listened as the women continued reminiscing about who was best at ironing altar linens, who made the best casserole, who loved to bring buckets of chrysanthemums to the flower guild each fall. They mentioned Diane, very much still alive and active, who loved to care for the church flower beds.

Diane and I had spoken recently. Her voice warbled as she said, "I worship mostly outdoors."

"That makes you the canonical Pacific Northwesterner," I said into the phone, assuming she was talking about the common regional preference for hiking over church.

"No, I love church. I mean that my favorite thing to do at church is pull weeds outside. I helped to put in the rain gardens."

The church had collaborated several years earlier with a local organization that helped communities turn portions of their parking lots into bioswales filled with water-loving plants. The rain gardens at Saints Peter & Paul were often receptacles for empty beer cans and other trash not easy to remove when they were filled with water.

"I wish I could get out there again," Diane was saying, "but during the pandemic I've been really getting into my own garden."

I assured her that God was there, too.

There was something I had hoped to hear in the Zoom call with the women I had identified as the church matriarchs that I wasn't hearing. I had this idea that the church held in its history a traceable lineage of powerful women, women who ran the church despite the centuries-old tradition of male priests about whom church ladies would regularly say "Father knows best."

What I was learning from this conversation and others like it is that unlike the matriarchs in my family, the ladies of my church lived to pour themselves out for others, and to pass on traditions I later decided were more significant than a jeweled silver spoon. The traditions were ones of attention to detail, love for one another, remembering (or at least acknowledging) birthdays, keeping things beautiful for future generations and always, always making sure that people had enough to eat, whether the people were Sunday school students in need of snacks, a priest in need of breakfast, or houseless men and women in need of a takeout dinner.

The women I spoke with, keepers of the parish history, would not have spoken in a language of power and influence, and would not have said that power was part of their legacy. And yet, there it was, precisely because they were the ones to tell the stories. They were the ones I asked.

I wanted the women of Saints Peter & Paul to have the power they deserved in their little church. I suspected that none of my male clergy predecessors in that place would have thought about giving power away to these ladies. This meant swimming upstream in the Father-knows-best culture that persisted, even in 2020.

I felt a rush of gratitude for the men who had taught me, men who had opted out of the traditional power structures in each of their contexts and divested themselves of any patriarchal birthright. Instead, they each left space in themselves for what some might call "the divine feminine."

I would call it radical hospitality of the heart.

Chapter 4

Open

O n March 20, 2020, women who lived in tents, cars, and nearby low-income housing arrived at Saints Peter & Paul as they had every Friday for nearly twenty years. In the parking lot they found the usual security guard, John, along with the Multnomah County needle exchange van which had been a Friday fixture at the church even longer than Rahab's Sisters, a Friday night gathering of women on the margins. Volunteers greeted them outside, which was unusual, but not as unusual as the sight of them all wearing masks and gloves.

The big door leading from the parking lot to the church's fellowship hall and kitchen—considered, as in most churches, the "main door" even though it was farthest from the worship space—was propped open but blocked by a large round table. Gloved volunteers handed to-go boxes of hot soup across the table. I stood next to a regular volunteer named Kaylyn, a twenty-something architect who was laid off from her job when her office closed due to COVID-19. I envied her hair, which had been dyed vermillion some months ago, and was dark on top with a grow-out that blended with red and pale pink at the ends. I loved how bright hair color was everywhere in Portland and hated that it just doesn't stick to gray hair, no matter how much you bleach it out first.

I could hear random comments from the guests that reminded me that not everyone began their day scrolling through New York Times headlines as I did.

"Everything is closed! Why is everything closed?" asked a large woman wearing hot pink leggings and flip-flops. I'd seen her before at various times of year. Always flip-flops.

"Did you hear about that flu, covid-something?" muttered the person standing in front of her, rummaging for cigarettes.

"This'll be the first food I've had in two days. Meals on Wheels usually comes on Fridays, but I waited and waited, and they never showed." This from an older woman who was a long-time regular at Rahab's Sisters; normally, she came more for the social life than anything else.

"I think my neighbor's real sick," said a friend standing beside her.

"Everyone looks so weird with their masks."

"We thought you would be closed."

Karin, who provided mental health counseling, climbed out of her SUV and greeted one of the women lined up waiting for food. She pulled her mask off for a few seconds. "It's me! You'll have to know by my eyes that I'm smiling."

Those first days and weeks of the pandemic were confusing, especially to people living outside, without the constant access to information most of us took for granted. While grocery stores—considered essential—never closed, food banks and most non-profits providing services to houseless people did close, either for health and safety reasons or what nonprofit boards liked to call "risk management," a euphemism for the fear of being sued.

Schools and libraries closed, coffee shops closed, Meals on Wheels ceased deliveries, and Lyft and Uber drivers stayed home. For most businesses and almost all social services, being closed became the norm. Rahab's Sisters was different. While some of the regular volunteers dropped off the Friday night rotation, others increased their efforts, coming every Friday, often bringing family members with them. Instead of doing less, Rahab's Sisters did more. They collected more clothing and supplies than ever before and handed them out by the hundreds each week. When they heard that people living outside were going hungry because so many services were shut down, Rahab's Sisters volunteers began taking meals to homeless camps on Sunday nights by caravan.

The inspiration for Rahab's Sisters was a street outreach in the East End of London called the Maze Marigold project. For six weeks in the summer of 2002 my family and I lived with Father Brian Ralph, his wife Tracy, and their two daughters, Sinead (thirteen) and Siobhan (three). I learned about East London, and its rich history of church outreach to poor immigrants and people living on the margin, by following Father Brian around. The rhythm of each day was set by morning prayer in the church, afternoon tea in the vicarage kitchen, and an evening pint at the local pub. By night I witnessed a quality of interaction and support for vulnerable women I'd never seen or even imagined.

Maze Marigold got part of its name from an existing neighborhood outreach to IV drug users called "The Maze." "Marigold" was a household word in England for a brand of ladies' rubber gloves, the kind our mothers might've worn for washing dishes or scrubbing floors. The name linked the street experience of the women and girls served by the Maze Marigold Project to the everyday experiences of women like my mother, women with homes and families.

I don't think I ever wore rubber gloves to wash dishes, but I'd washed my share, especially while I was in seminary and my husband did all the cooking. With my home and family, I was on the "everyday" end of the spectrum of women's experience as measured by polite society, but my husband understood my eagerness to cross the Atlantic for an immersive experience with vulnerable women at the other end of the spectrum.

On the plane to London on a June night, we sat three across: my husband at the window, our five-year-old nestled between us clutching his child-sized backpack full of books, and me on the aisle where I could easily get up and walk off my traveler's nerves. As people finished their evening meal and pulled on blankets and eyeshades, I searched my own memories and associations with sex work. There was the year or two I spent volunteering at the jail under the bible-thumping tutelage of the seasoned prison chaplain. Before that, in college, there were two tangential experiences of my own, which I'd filed away into the recesses of my mind for a very long time.

There was a time, when, living off campus, drinking heavily, and financially desperate, I couldn't bear to tell my parents once again that I was out of money. I considered sleeping with my sleazy, married landlord in lieu of paying rent. He was a fortyish guy who'd lived in that college town his whole life and had played on the high school football team. He wore too-tight khakis and golf sweaters and hung out at the same bar that I did. But I had a hard time even imagining a conversation with him that lasted for more than the thirty seconds of pleasantries we would exchange over loud disco music, let alone whatever conversation would lead to an exchange of sex for rent relief.

But the thought experiment took me closer to an edge than I'd been before, and opened a window on the desperation of women without the safety net of family or trusted, gainfully employed friends. My own experiences of blackout drinking and waking up in the wrong beds made it easy to see through that window. The recollection of that time, that particular edge, made me shudder for my nineteen-year-old beer-soaked self and for young women who found themselves vulnerable and desperate.

In the dark airplane cabin, I remembered my college friend Alice, whose experience was as deeply etched in my memory as if it were my own.

It was 1979. Alice and I lay crashed out on her bed, having spent a warm spring afternoon drinking beer and getting stoned. A rap on the window woke me up. The window faced the back porch and Melanie, who lived downstairs, stood out on the porch banging her keyring. "Al, wake up. You need to call Pearl. Right now."

Alice got up, reaching for her hairbrush the way she always did.

"What's that about?" I asked. "Who's Pearl?"

"She runs an escort service out by the mall."

Brush, brush, tilting her head toward the brush on one side and then the other. Her hair got shinier as she brushed, the color of chestnut. "I'm gonna go sleep with a guy for a hundred dollars."

That woke me up.

"You can stay here," Alice said. "I'm gonna hit the shower."

Then she went.

I was horrified. I couldn't say anything. The old pipes of her apartment building clanged and squeaked as she ran the shower. *Why didn't you ask your friends for money?* This is what I wanted to say. *What about your career after graduation, everything you've worked for? What if you run into one of these bozos in your office someday?* And yet, without any work or concrete plan for a career after graduation, I was living on that same edge. But working for Pearl seemed to cross the line. And it was Alice! Ms. Perfect straight A student.

As her clogs clattered down the stairs, I imagined a businessman with pomade hair, bursting shirt buttons, and bad skin waiting in a hotel bar for my energetic straight-A friend.

I hadn't heard Pearl's name before, but I knew all about the escort services that regularly advertised in our local college-town paper. *Escorts needed for out-of-town guests. No experience necessary.* I could picture Alice in one of the motel rooms near the new South Hadley mall, smoothing her skirt as she stood up to respond to a knock, reaching for her hairbrush one last time. Or maybe she would be the one knocking at the motel room door, a voluminous handbag over her shoulder. A twinge of anger pricked at me mid-picture. *He doesn't deserve you. Don't do it!*

Alice's experience taught me that as readily as I once climbed into bed with classmates or mutual friends at the drop of a few beers or a compliment, I was a chicken when it came to getting undressed for a trucker I'd never met. It seemed to cross a line, and at the same time, the idea filled me with dread, because it had seemed that the possibility was right around the corner.

Twenty-three years later, on the airplane hurtling through space toward our London adventure, I wasn't threatened by financial or sexual vulnerability like Alice had been back then, but the memories were fresh in my mind. The memories faded over the first days in London as I recovered from jet lag, navigated the neighborhood that would be home for six weeks, and got to know our host family.

A week into our stay in the East End, my memories of Alice's experiences came back the first night I was to go out with the Maze Marigold project. Rayna, one of the two women who ran the program, picked me up in a white minivan. We drove to their office to meet Angela, the other half of the Maze Marigold duo whom Brian had told me about.

We parked in the alley behind a residential street a few blocks from the always-bustling Whitechapel Road. Rayna locked up the van and then unlocked the door to what looked like a garage.

"Here we'll get our supplies ready and then head out. Angela'll be along in a moment." I decided not to ask any questions and just let the evening unfold.

Rayna had close-cropped hair, white at the roots. She had a wide smile and warm laugh that put me at ease. She had the thick arms and shoulders of someone who'd grown up working outdoors on a farm in one of England's rural counties, maybe with a baby or toddler on each hip.

Angela showed up about thirty seconds later.

Angela had long, dark hair and bangs that made her eyes pop. She came to the Maze as an office volunteer when her children left home and was hired after a government grant funded two paid staff positions. She initially struck me as the quieter of the two women. As I came to know her, I found she was the more perceptive—dogged in her approach to the women and girls who made up the Maze clientele. Both Rayna and Angela looked to be in their late 40s. Not much older than me, but both had grown children and a substantive toughness to them.

"The first thing is to sort the condoms." Rayna pronounced it "con-DOMS" with her East End accent. Angela put two large cardboard boxes on the long 1950s laminate table that filled most of the small kitchen-turned-office, along with a stack of small wax paper bags, the kind you'd slip a cookie-to-go into, except these were dark green.

"These here come from the government," Angela said, pointing to the larger of the two cartons, "And these we buy ourselves, with grant money. Same as the van." She now had her back to me as she spoke, running water in the sink while pulling insulated coffee carafes down from a high shelf.

"Twenty condoms per baggie, see? Twelve flavored, eight non," added Rayna, but she said "tweh-ie."

The government-issue condoms were flavorless and came in grey packages with black and white print. The purchased ones were flavored and color-coded. Yellow for banana, pink for strawberry, brown for chocolate, yellow and white stripes for piña colada. Who knew? I sat there sorting the condoms, not only following Rayna's instructions but also putting equal numbers of the different flavors in each little sack, I thought about what a difference it might make, to someone who gave blow jobs all night long, to mask the sterile rubbery taste with something sweet.

Angela and Rayna took their time getting ready to go out in the van. They got a kick out of the shy seminarian playing with condoms.

"Aw, ain't that nice?" said Angela. "She's making sure each girl gets a piña colada in her bag."

"Piña colada; that's their favorite," said Rayna. "Funny, since 'alf of 'em ain't old enough to drink."

Angela and Rayna made small talk while we organized supplies, swapping stories about their day. They also shared stories about Father Brian, who had helped to start the Maze Marigold Project five years earlier. One of Rayna's favorite stories was about a sex worker who asked her: "Is he a proper priest, or d'ya suppose he'd fancy a go?" Brian didn't really look like a "proper priest" with his spiky hair and Doc Martins, but for the sex worker's intention, he was.

After we sorted condoms, we drove out of the quiet residential neighborhood into Whitechapel Road and pulled up along a dark intersection near Spitalfields Market. The street looked abandoned. Angela parked the van with a little lurch. We got out, opened up the back, and righted the carafes full of coffee and hot water. I rearranged some of the sandwiches on a plastic platter, thrilled to have something to do while we waited.

The first woman came from an alley I hadn't even seen when we pulled up. She wore tight jeans and dark glasses. I wondered how she could see. The air was still and heavy. There was traffic noise from a few blocks away, but where we were parked, it was quiet enough to hear the clack-clack of heels approaching the van, as another woman came out of the shadows, long ropey hair shrouding her face. They looked hungry, but both were more interested in coffee and condoms than food.

They chatted with Rayna and Angela as if they'd run into them at Starbucks, complimenting each other on their outfits, reporting on their current living situation, and asking after mutual friends.

My job was to stand on the curb near the back of the van to hand out sandwiches and pour coffee.

"Encourage them to eat a sandwich *before* they have a bunch of coffee," Rayna had said. "But don't push them. And don't be surprised at how much sugar they want. It's the heroin does that to them."

It was true. I'd pour them some coffee, add some cream, and offer sugar. No one took fewer than four packets; several took five or six. I learned to open the packets three at a time the way truckers did, tapping them like a syringe before tearing off three tops in unison. I considered it a great triumph if one of the ladies ate a sandwich in front of me. That was their supper, standing around the hatch of the van. I was equally happy when one of the women took another sandwich and put it in her handbag, until Angela explained that she would probably have to give that one to her pimp or to some other man who was not welcome at the Maze van.

"Where are you staying these days?" Angela asked a girl named Valerie.

Valerie was spider leg-thin, with wisps for hair. Her tight jeans stopped at her calves. A man's shirt hung on bony shoulders, a faded grey tank top underneath. A large handbag hung on her shoulder.

"Oh, it's real nice. Well, not nice really, but I've got the place to myself. Right over there," she waved with her cigarette. "Two streets over. It's cool."

As the conversation unfolded, it turned out Valerie was actually sleeping in a "lift," the elevator of an abandoned building. To her it was safe and private; she could control who came and went.

I thought about Hans Christian Andersen's Little Match Girl, freezing to death on the street before elevators existed, before the Match Girl's strike a few blocks from where we stood. Maybe sleeping in a lift wasn't as bad as it sounded.

Years later during one pandemic winter and then another, I learned about how people in tents kept warm and the risks and complications of scant emergency warming shelters. It was a miracle more people didn't freeze to death on the streets.

"You still like your flat?" Angela was saying to a ghost-white girl with stringy black hair. She sometimes went by Deb, and sometimes Charlene. She wore white jeans and a black cowboy shirt with cracked mother-of-pearl snaps.

"Oh yes. Well, it's getting a little crowded. My boyfriend moved in. Then his sister. Then this other girl." Angela and Rayna looked at each other and Rayna rolled her eyes. After Deb-who-sometimes-went-by-Charlene wandered off into the dark with a sandwich, Rayna explained to me that "boyfriend" meant pimp. Deb had lost the little bit of independence she might've found in having her own place.

Most of the women were heroin addicts. Their boyfriends gave them the drugs in order to keep them dependent, and then pimped them out. All they had in common were drugs and bad teeth. And how thin they were. Bone skinny, with knobby wrists showing when I handed them their sweet coffee.

The exceptions were three Afro-Caribe women. I saw them across the intersection, coming out of the dark like the others, but with a difference. They didn't look hungry; they strutted and swaggered, costume jewelry glinting under the streetlight. By day, they studied real estate at the local equivalent of a community college, and they planned to go into business together when they were done with their schooling. They didn't do drugs and didn't have pimps. They wore short shorts and tight tops that showed off generous curves. They shared a flat together, and they looked out for one another. They brought their loud laughter into the small circle of girl-women gathered around the van. More than anyone else I saw that evening, these women matched a stereotypical image of a hooker: they were in their mid-20s and wore flashy, bright clothing, lots of make-up, high heels. But they were in the minority. The women we saw over the evening ranged in age from 15 to 50. Their hair was short, long, or in between. Most wore little or no make-up. A few wore high heels, but most wore Converse or ballet slippers. Letting go of my notions of what prostituted women looked like was one of the lessons of the evening.

"Thanks, love," said one to me when I handed her a sandwich.

"Hey, sugar," said another to a rail-thin girl cupping her coffee for warmth. "You know if you put weight on those bones, you wouldn't be cold on such a warm night."

Her friends laughed, each munching happily on day-old turkey and swiss. The one she called "Sugar" gave a half-smile, empty as her stomach.

When I was her age—maybe 19—I wanted nothing more than to be skinny like Sugar. In high school I had been secretly jealous of a girl named Heather, who was repeatedly hospitalized for anorexia. If someone told me I could get to look like that by shooting a lot of heroin, I might almost have done it. One of a series of near misses in my life.

The gathering under the streetlight in the otherwise dark intersection felt like a weekly reunion of a sort. The unlikely space where all women were welcome offered the women something I sensed they didn't get any-where else, a quality of hospitality I would not have expected, had my life taken the turns their lives had.

There was also something tough about these young women that my younger self would have envied. When I was an adolescent, I had all of the vulnerability they had, with none of the tough talk or the emotional armor that was supposed to keep them from getting hurt. At 40-something, I could see that their toughness was just part of their vulnerability and sadness. The women evoked in me not envy but love and the longing to connect.

There was a girl named Lindy, who met a regular every Tuesday at the Whitechapel Burger King. She'd show up at one of our stops and we'd give her a ride.

Angela usually drove; Rayna turned around and made conversation with Lindy. "How's your mum?"

"Oh, the same. We had tea before I came out tonight. She's good."

Lindy looked more put-together than most of the girls, with shiny clean hair brushed neatly over her shoulders, dark jeans, and a leather jacket zipped up to her collarbone.

"Aren't you warm?" Rayna asked.

"I've just got a vest on under." I didn't see the vest. In England, a vest is what we Americans call a camisole.

Each week, Lindy and I rode together in the back seat in silence. I was increasingly aware of all the things women like Lindy heard their whole lives and learned not to believe, about God, about love and care, about hope. There was something steely about her eyes and her shoulders, square against her seat, poised for a quick exit. Putting a hand on her bony shoulder and saying "Jesus loves you" or "I'm here for you" would not reach her. What would reach her? Perhaps just showing up, week after week, as Angela and Rayna did.

"G'night, then," Lindy said as we pulled up in front of Burger King.

"You take care!" called Rayna after her.

Rayna's jaw was set tough whenever she said goodbye to any of the women, especially the young ones, her cheek twitching. I watched Lindy disappear inside, curious what her regular Tuesday night date looked like. What kind of man would want to meet each Tuesday at Burger King at 8:30 at night? What would they do? Eat a couple of Whoppers and go to his nearby bedsit? Go out a back door to have sex in his car before he went home to his family? Would this be the time he beat her? Would she brush her hair afterwards and go back on the street? Call Angela for a ride? Go home to make a nightcap for her mum?

Come home with me, I wanted to say. *We'll have tea, we'll talk, we'll go shopping, we'll be friends, I'll tell you about America, I'll come meet your mum, buy you some shirts so you can unzip your jacket, tell you how pretty your hair is.* I wanted to run after Lindy, grab her bony wrist, hold her small, rough hand in mine. I longed to be her mother, pastor and friend all rolled into one. But I was glued to my seat, the car door heavy and impenetrable between us. The anger and incredulity I felt years before about Alice's desperation was gone. Instead, I longed for connection, longed to be a bearer of some small hope.

The East End of London left a mark on me, and I was hooked. After returning home, I pined for the neighborhood with its profusion of cheap Bengali food, open air markets, and cultural and religious diversity. I missed being on the streets at night alongside the Maze Project volunteers I'd met there.

⊕

Newly ordained in Portland a year later, I loved being a priest. But I soon wearied of the complaints of the affluent churchgoers whose spiritual lives I was paid to support. I didn't care that the children's choir director was overly brusque with little Bobby when he told her about his soccer game, or that the St. Nicholas Party I'd planned conflicted with a school orchestra event. I should have cared, perhaps, but I didn't.

This was in the fall of 2003. I was working as an assistant priest in a thriving parish that served about a hundred affluent families and couples in a comfortable neighborhood in Northeast Portland. I did all the things that new assistant priests do: I managed the Sunday school, hosted newcomer dinners, preached on Christmas morning and the Sunday after Easter, and learned everything I could about running a church. Stephen, who had been my priest and mentor when I began the ordination process, was now my boss. He was as wise and kind as ever, but my heart was elsewhere.

I had looked half-heartedly for programs in Portland that offered the kind of no-strings-attached hospitality and nonjudgmental care I'd witnessed in East London. I found nothing.

"I want to make a difference to someone's *real life*," I routinely whined to my husband. I longed for time on the streets and gritty interaction with women whose daily lives were a matter of life and death.

"I think you should give this a shot," Mark would say. "You haven't been at this long enough to know what's the right fit at the right time." He was sensible and pragmatic about such things. He told me to be patient. He reminded me to be thankful I had landed a paying job at a time when not all new seminary graduates could.

I was forty-four then, just beginning to claim "middle aged" for myself, but I was still a new priest. I hadn't yet sat with someone while they died, or while they grieved the death of their child. I hadn't yet presided at the dozen funerals that would come my way in the next year. I didn't yet understand how many ways I could make a difference in someone's life.

At a clergy meeting in October of that year, listening to a national church bureaucrat who had flown in from New York to talk to us about hunger statistics in Oregon, I started doodling and daydreaming. I imagined a "midnight mass for working women" at the little Episcopal church on 82nd Avenue, the closest thing Portland had to a red-light district, a four-lane boulevard along the eastern edge of the city, with a mile-long section the police call *the track*, where sex workers walked up and down, twenty or thirty minutes each way in bad shoes, passing pawn shops, car dealers, motels, strip clubs, Asian restaurants, and one church.

A new friend, Ellie, had just been called as the assistant priest at that church. It was the first time a woman had served there, and her coming had shaken the congregation just enough that it might not be too much of a step from there to some kind of street ministry to sex workers, using the church hall as a base.

I shared my idea with Ellie, and I talked with her about the Maze Project. She told me that she had worked in a halfway house for street women in Washington, DC before beginning seminary. Later that afternoon, we talked about our newly hatched idea over tea with a group of clergywomen at the conference: a drop-in center in the church's fellowship hall that would open late and offer women a safe place to visit with other women and have a hot meal. We didn't have a clear plan; we knew only that we would offer non-judgmental hospitality. We thought we'd begin with one Friday each month.

The idea caught the imagination of several of the women.

Maryanne, a tiny woman with twinkly sapphires for eyes who had been a priest for thirty years, said: "I think this is what I've been praying for!"

Anita, a priest in a small town too far away to participate, suggested: "You could wash their feet."

In ancient Palestine, guests who had traveled a long journey would have their feet washed by their host's servant when they arrived, or by their host, if he had no servant. In the Bible, Jesus washed his disciples' feet before he died, as a sign of the servant ministry he wanted them to imitate. In some Christian traditions, people wash each other's feet on Maundy Thursday, the night that commemorates the Last Supper. Anita's idea gave me goosebumps.

More ideas began to fly around the room as we sipped tea and ate cucumber sandwiches and cake.

"You could get medical students to volunteer and do basic health screening."

"Someone could give them haircuts for free. Or massages."

"Get a dentist's office to donate toothbrushes or come and do dental check-ups."

"Starbucks would donate day-old pastry."

"My church could knit prayer shawls for the ladies."

Everyone wanted to help. Everyone wanted to reach out to prostituted women on the street and love them.

By the end of the conversation, a core group of six of us had formed, and the other five seemed to be looking to me for leadership. I felt energy and ideas buzzing through my body like caffeine. I barely skated over sleep that night, and when I did finally drift off, I woke up making notes of our new program, although it had neither approval from the board of Saints Peter & Paul, nor a name.

Things moved quickly, and this seemed to be a sign that we were doing something right. The church board approved the Friday night venture, with its usual mix of generosity and trepidation. At our second meeting, just weeks after that October clergywomen's tea, we landed on a name.

"What about Rahab's Daughters?" suggested a red-headed deacon named Marla.

"Yes" and "Oh, yes!" others replied.

I had long been a fan of Rahab but suggested "Rahab's Sisters" instead.

The others agreed that the ambiguity in "who is helping whom" worked well. In the final consensus we were all "sisters."

Rahab, often called "Rahab the Harlot," lived and worked in what was probably a violent neighborhood on the edge of the ancient city of Jericho. People who lived on the edge, like Rahab, inhabited two worlds: the world of the city and the world of the desert. Portland's 82nd Avenue was like that, a dividing line between the city and what was through the last decade of the twentieth century a no-man's-land, violent and seedy, a place where most Portlanders did not go out at night.

We made up quarter-sheet fliers on pink paper:

On the streets?

Need a bite to eat or a cup of hot cocoa?

Want a warm, safe place for a few minutes?

Take a break! Women of all faiths and women of no faith are invited to stop in . . . .

What: A hot meal to stay or to go, a hot drink, clean restrooms, companionship, health products, and prayers if you want them

When: Every other Friday (1st, 3rd, 5th), 7–11 pm

Where: Saints Peter & Paul Episcopal Church (SE 82nd between Stark and Burnside—enter through parking lot on Ash)

Open

Women only! Women only! Women Only! Women Only!

I found myself buying a lot of pink. Pink paper to print fliers on, pink underwear, pink candles, pink-iced cookies. We put pink in our official logo when we finally got around to having one. Why pink? Just as many of these women and girls had been robbed of their childhood, I felt like they probably didn't have much connection with femininity that hadn't been misused or abused. Nothing said feminine like pink. Some of the other volunteers thought it was cheesy, but I stuck to my pink guns.

We distributed the fliers to the motels that lined much of 82nd Avenue, and stuck them inside payphones.[1]

On a dark and rainy December night in 2003, we prayed first for eyes to see women who might otherwise be invisible to us. We prayed to uphold the principle of hospitality attributed to the fifth century St. Benedict: welcome all guests as if they were Christ. A couple of us walked up and down 82nd Avenue in the rain with huge golf umbrellas, greeting women we saw and inviting them to stop by the church with the light on. Other volunteers waited eagerly inside the church's fellowship hall, standing like maîtres d' next to a cornucopia of chocolate, ladies underwear, warm socks, homemade cookies, coffee (and sugar packets), and hot soup.

The first week: one woman came in. Then the next week: two. The week after that: five. Then three, then seven, then four, then six. It reminded me of starting a church: the growth is never what you expect, and you need to change your plans along the way.

The volunteers in those early days were mostly clergywomen like me, or our trusted friends, like Carol. Carol and I had met at the county's Center for Community Justice, where she ran a program to help people released from jail to get their GED and apply for jobs. As I worked alongside Carol as a volunteer teaching people to read, we became friends. When Rahab's Sisters started up, I knew I wanted Carol there with me. She was tough and sweet, brave and honest. We had shared conversations about faith. She was Mennonite, which meant that she brought an unwavering sense of justice mixed with hospitality to everything she did.

"People associate the Mennonites with a whole lot of shunning," she said to me once over lunch. "And there has been. But we don't go in for that so much anymore."

---

1. In 2003 many people had cell phones, but not everyone. In particular, sex workers whose every possession was under the control of a pimp rarely had their own phones.

I had asked Carol to be the chaplain for our group of volunteers, some-one who would lead us in prayer at the beginning and end of each evening. We were all clergywomen then, but we wanted someone from outside our customary circle to pray with us. Carol was the right person, because she saw so many sides to life, and brought all of this to her prayers for us and for the women on the street. She cried when I asked her and cried again when she said yes.

Carol brought her friend JoAnne. Like Carol, JoAnne was Mennonite. They loved to bring food with them, and their compassion was deep. They were earnest, nervous (despite their best efforts) about being in a dangerous neighborhood, and devoted to the possibility of helping people, especially if it involved home cooking.

Being back in Portland in 2020 after five years away, and back at Saints Peter & Paul as a parish priest this time, I had a front-row seat at Rahab's Sisters ongoing presence on the corner of 82nd and Ash, as well as many occasions to reflect back on those early years. That quintessential 2020 pandemic word, *pivot*, applied to Rahab's Sisters in its first years as well. Eventually, women came regularly for the hot meal, the new underwear, and the hygiene supplies. Our list of essentials grew as we began to get to know the women we served and their needs.

"Do you have any big bottles of shampoo?" one woman asked one Friday. "The little ones . . . they're like what you get on a date in a skeezy motel. I want something like, you know, like I'd have at home."

"Do you have any make-up?" asked a young woman whose dark stringy hair hung down over one side of her face, covering a bruise. From then on, we stocked eye shadow along with four different shades of founda-tion and concealer.

Over the next sixteen years, Rahab's Sisters grew. Each week we had more guests, and more volunteers sought us out as a way to connect with the growing number of women. The sex trafficking of young women and girls made it into the local news with increasing regularity, and this was a draw for many of our volunteers and prospective funders. We incorpo-rated as a separate not-for-profit organization so that we could apply for grants from larger non-church donors. Although we occasionally dreamt big dreams of expanding in the direction of residential treatment and em-ployment programs outside the city, we always returned to the reality that what we offered seemed to be unique, and Christian in all the right ways: unconditional welcome, no-strings-attached hospitality, and an experience of rest and community most of the women who came to us missed in the rest of their lives.

I had come across other churches trying to help women who made their living on the street. There were always strings attached. Representatives from other groups wanted to rescue vulnerable women, to take them out of their environment and preach them into wanting a better life. The only path they offered, however, was Jesus, and maybe a gift card to the local Goodwill for some clean clothes.

I liked to think that I was a friend to Jesus, a follower, even, but I knew there was more to helping the women on the street than to get them to love Jesus. Especially because some of them had such bad experiences with God and church growing up.

Our volunteers over the years came into Rahab's Sisters wondering whether we would be preaching to our guests, trying to convert them. At volunteer trainings, someone would inevitably ask:

"What do I say to them?"

"You say: 'How do you take your coffee? May I get you anything else?' Think about it. I doubt anyone has asked them that for a long time."

It turned out that treating sex workers and intravenous drug users like ordinary women was the hospitality they needed most.

There was more to it, of course. We discouraged volunteers from asking whether guests were married or had children—the normal small talk of privileged people—because those were almost always complicated and painful subjects.

"Let *them* bring up their kids. If you sit with them long enough, they almost always will."

We taught volunteers that what we offered was a quality of interaction, a quality of hospitality that transcended faith or any common beliefs, but got to the heart of the best kinds of spiritual experience: radical hospitality.

Originally developed as an outreach to female sex workers, Rahab's Sisters expanded to include all women "marginalized by the sex industry, homelessness, poverty, or drug addiction," and eventually to "anyone whose gender identity makes them vulnerable." By 2020 Rahab's Sisters had an Executive Director, three paid staff members, a mental health counseling presence each Friday, and dozens of energetic volunteers. The offerings were always the same: a hot house-made meal, hygiene supplies, and a warm, dry place to be with friends and let others serve coffee and hot soup.

The first time I went out with Rahab's Sisters on a Sunday night I was part of a team of three cars going to the central strip of the bike corridor that lined I-205, the interstate that rings the city. Small encampments regularly sprang up along the bike path, usually "swept" by police every few weeks. During the first months of the pandemic, however, police ceased their sweeps, both to protect themselves from COVID-19 and because there were no COVID-safe alternatives. Living outside, while perilous for many reasons, might have been seen as a form of protection against the virus from people who would otherwise be in a crowded shelter or jail.

"Sara, you take the hot food," said Kaylyn, sweeping her arm toward half a dozen coolers and open cartons of brown to-go boxes. "Liz, you'll take the snack bags. I'll take the water and everything else."

Volunteers loaded the back of my Subaru with the coolers and open cardboard boxes filled with meals. The smell of home-made macaroni and cheese wafted up at me. The boxes were hot on the bottom. I knew the people we were bringing it to didn't get a lot of hot meals, especially not delivered to their tent.

The first site was a small one, two tents next to a busy street that crossed the freeway overpass. The bike path widened to meet the street; the tents were pitched in the triangle formed by the path's on-ramp, a neighbor's fence, and the sidewalk. From each tent hung large blue tarps covering a multitude of belongings: bicycles, suitcases, lawn chairs, and even a lawn mower.

"Hello!" Kaylyn called out as we approached. "Anybody home?"

There was no one in sight.

"Dinner! Anybody want some dinner?"

A fifty-something guy came walking up the bike path ramp. In the warm summer night, he wore a T-shirt with a plaid flannel shirt and polyester vest on top of that.

"Hey, Henry! I've been worried about you!" Kaylyn gave him a quick hug. "Want some dinner?

"Yes, ma'am," said Henry, who seemed otherwise to be a man of few words.

"Do you know where the others are?"

"Haven't seen 'em. Lots of folks gone swimming this afternoon. So hot." There was a city bus that traveled from near where we stood all the way southeast out of the city to the Clackamas River. During every summer hot spell, the newspapers reported deaths of people who drowned from the shock of icy snow-melt water compared to the heat. Often the bodies pulled from the river were hard to identify. I realized it was probably because they lived without address, without identification, and without family. Now, without enough food, social services or even police, they were perhaps even more vulnerable.

"If we leave some food for them, will you make sure they get it?" I put down four of the warm boxes just outside one of the tents. Kaylyn handed him a couple of gallons of water, while Liz set down several snack bags containing cereal bars, utensils for the hot meal, a couple of juice boxes, a roll of toilet paper, bottle of hand sanitizer, a pair of masks, and a miniature first aid kit.

"Sometimes, we bring the hospitality to them," Kaylyn said.

The Rahab's Sisters volunteers did not identify as parishioners of Saints Peter & Paul nor even, in most instances, as Christians. And yet, this traveling hospitality, which included no bible, no prayers, no priestly wisdom from me or anyone else, was a way of being church. Radical hospitality meant showing up for the poorest of the poor, wherever they are. Like the white van showing up every Wednesday and Friday in the dark intersections behind bustling Whitechapel Road in East London, Rahab's Sisters was open. It's what was meant to happen.

Chapter 5

Setting a Table in the Wilderness

I *think we need to draw a line in the asphalt*, read the first line of an email Linda sent. The occasion was that I'd allowed a man to set up his tent, tarps, and a shopping cart's worth of belongings in a corner of the church parking lot. Linda was too sweet and soft-spoken to confront me in person or even on the phone in what was to be our first disagreement. I'd been at the church for about three weeks. The email made my stomach lurch, just a bit. I never liked making unpopular decisions.

How this started was that one of the volunteers from Rahab's Sisters had written to me about Kevin: *He's new in town, just got out of the hospital, and just needs a place to camp for a few nights. He feels safe near the church.*

It seemed fine to me. His tent fit neatly in the parking lot's so-called "smoking area" (only "so-called" because people smoked all over the parking lot). My husband and I stopped by one Saturday morning on our way in to record the church service.

"Hello? Hello? Kevin? You okay? Do you need anything?"

There was no answer. Mark pulled a blanket and pillow from the Goodwill-bound box that occupied a perpetual spot in the back of our Subaru and left them outside the tent. When we came back outside an hour later, both pillow and blanket were gone.

Linda's email was the first time I'd heard an argument against providing space for a tent on church property, but it would not be the last. It was, however, the last time I readily agreed to allow someone to stay.

We do a lot, Linda wrote. *We can't do everything. It has never ended well when we've allowed people to camp in the past.*

I was not comfortable walking back from providing hospitality to a guy named Kevin I'd never met. I put the situation out of my mind for a few days until I got a call the following weekend from a neighborhood police officer.

"Yeah . . . " Why did certain people always begin their phone conversations that way? "We've gotten calls from a neighbor complaining about someone camping and making noise over there at your church. Do you know about this?"

"I know there's someone in the parking lot. I don't know about the complaints."

"Well, apparently one of your neighbors isn't too happy."

"Can you tell me which neighbor it was?" I asked.

"No, ma'am, sorry, I can't."

I don't know why I'd even asked the question. I knew which neighbor it was. I'd heard about Dale, who had moved up from Texas a few years earlier with his young family. He didn't like finding needles on the sidewalk in front of his house and I understood that. But he was part of a local group that had a reputation for harassing houseless people and talking about *cleaning up the neighborhood* as though humans were trash. Dale sometimes took pictures of women lined up outside the church on Rahab's Sisters' nights. I hadn't met him, but I'd heard he was a creep.

The cop continued, "I just need to know the church's policy on camping."

This was my opportunity to figure out whether I was going to push back on a parish faithful matriarch like Linda, or adopt for myself the no-camping policy that had worked for a long time. In the silence that ensued while I was deciding which way to go, the officer added, "If you are in charge and you tell me that no camping is allowed, then when a neighbor calls and complains I can take care of it without having to interrupt your Saturday afternoon."

"I don't like it, but I think that needs to be our policy, yes," I finally said.

"Okay, we'll take care of it."

I needed to learn that one can practice radical hospitality and set limits at the same time. And nothing was going to be perfect. I was glad to be doing what I knew the church ladies wanted, and at the same time I was concerned for Kevin. I put him out of my mind for the moment.

"How are you fine ladies doing on this fine evening?" The question came from a guy in cargo shorts who sauntered up to the table where I was helping a couple of women from the church hand out sandwiches. We were all in our sixties, so we were happy to be called "fine ladies." His silver hair was pulled back into a messy ponytail and a cigarette dangled from his maskless mouth.

"I haven't met you before," he said to me, moving his cigarette from the corner of his mouth to a spot between his nicotine-stained index and middle fingers. As he did so, I noticed the city dirt under his uncut fingernails. His eyes, though, were blue as a summer sky glittering above a clear mountain lake in July.

"I'm Sara, the new pastor here." We don't typically say *pastor* in the Episcopal Church, but I used it on the street because it's a generic term everyone understands.

"I'll remember that; my daughter's name is Sara. I'm Mark."

"I'll remember that," I replied. "My husband and my brother are both named Mark."

"Most people remember me by my last name," he said, leaning in a little more closely than I liked, especially since he wasn't wearing a mask. I held my breath. "It's Love. L-O-V-E, Love."

"I'll remember that one!" I was bad at names and hoped I was telling the truth.

For decades, Saints Peter & Paul served a meal on Tuesday nights to people living outside and in low-income apartments nearby. Our Tuesday night presence coincided with a needle exchange van that parked in the church parking lot twice each week on Tuesdays and Fridays. Run by the county's harm reduction unit, the needle van employees handed out clean needles and clean sharps containers to the neighborhood's many IV drug users. Harm reduction, not for the faint of heart, I always believed, was an act of recognition and compassion for people who lived dangerous and destructive lives in many ways. Some divine spark, some will to live, kept them showing up each week for clean needles and wound care supplies.

Brigid's Table had been a to-go meal of sack lunches for several years, although guests used to be invited inside to get their meal, use the restroom, and stock up on hygiene supplies. When the pandemic started, volunteers moved the meal outside, setting up a long folding table just outside the church entrance, and handing out sandwiches, water, and soda: turkey, ham, tuna salad, cheese, cola, root beer, lemon-lime.

This weekly offering was named Brigid's Table after St. Brigid of Kildare, who founded a monastic community in Kildare, Ireland, around 470 A.D. According to legend, the local King of Leinster promised Brigid as much land for her community as she could cover with her cloak. She lay the cloak on the ground and it grew and grew, eventually covering miles. Brigid's cloak became a metaphor for the reach the church wanted to have in serving the poor of its neighborhood.

The weekly volunteers were a couple of long-time members of the church, Sharon and Mary. Sharon, a widow who had been part of the church community for thirty years, was a short woman with the face of an owl and eyes that brightened whenever church conversation wandered to talk of feeding hungry people in our parish neighborhood. Her wobbly walk was all that remained of a bad stroke she had seven years earlier. She lived in a large ranch house in the suburbs and always had some combination of grandchildren, nieces, and nephews living with her.

Making sandwiches on Tuesday evenings was a passion for Sharon. She helped to fund the ministry each year and each week brought with her one or two grandchildren or another family member to help out. One of her nieces, Sally, regularly came with her on Tuesday nights. Sally had multicolored sleeve tattoos of tropical birds. *I just like them,* she had said when I asked her to tell me the story of her tattoos. She wore jeans that hugged her slim form and had rhinestone Vs on the back pockets. Her mask had rhinestones to match.

Sally was the one who rummaged through one of the several junk drawers in the church kitchen to find a roll of blue painter's tape and used it to make X's in the parking lot, six feet apart, so people who lined up for sandwiches could follow guidelines for social distancing during the pandemic. Even with the X's, Sally needed to monitor the line closely. Sharon said she enjoyed bossing the guys—it was mostly guys who came on Tuesday nights—around.

Mary had been part of the congregation for three or four years—a short-timer by church standards—but had been part of Portland-area Episcopal churches for all of her six decades. She brought a lot of wisdom and experience and also a lot of opinions. She moved slowly through the kitchen helping with the sandwiches. When they were ready, when Sally had put out the blue painter's tape and Sharon's grandson had piled the brown paper bags full of sandwiches and cookies in neat piles by the entrance, Mary took a seat next to the table. Her job was to ask each person who came to the door what they wanted to drink and put their choice of soda in their bag.

"Can I have two?" asked a wiry guy named Jack. "My girlfriend's in the car."

"Can I get two? I haven't eaten," said a guy named Jim with a sleeping bag draped over his broad shoulders.

We almost always gave out two sandwiches anyway.

"Can I get five?" asked a clean-shaven guy wearing a pea coat and towing a Radio Flier red wagon. Mary paused mid-bag, and gave him a look that said "really?" I could tell she was sizing up his clean-cut look along with his request.

"I got kids at home. We live in a construction trailer on Glisan."

She took his drink order and filled his bags. It took longer than the others and Sally reminded everyone else to stand on their blue Xs.

"Don't worry," she called out in her strong outdoor voice. "There'll be enough for everyone."

"Not if we give everyone five sandwiches," said Mary, to anyone who would listen.

"You're right," said Sharon, always the peacemaker. "I just don't think we've ever run out. Hey, Sally, have we ever run out?"

"Nah," said Sally. "Some weeks we think we're going to, but we don't."

I watched all this feeling grateful to witness this generosity. The outpouring of abundance—even with the blip-on-the-screen of scarcity which was the norm in many church circles—made my heart glad.

Most weeks there were sandwiches left over at eight, when the church volunteers closed up the kitchen and went home. The needle exchange van from the county stayed until nine, and so we gave all our leftover sandwiches to them and they handed them out to stragglers.

Mark L.O.V.E got his sandwiches, two turkey and two root beers, and we chatted some more at the edge of the parking lot. Most of the guys who came for sandwiches were not initially friendly, and I was glad to have met someone who was. I'd learned that there are a whole lot of normal small-talk questions that don't work for people on the streets. You don't ask where someone works, whether they have kids, or what part of town they live in.

"Where do you usually stay?" I asked, as I'd been taught years before by a homelessness outreach worker.

He told me he lived in his pickup truck which he parked around the corner in front of the large Methodist church that sat on a quiet residential street a block off our 82nd Avenue.

"I've lived in Montavilla my whole life," said Mark. "My mother, too. This is my home."

I knew that Mark Love was talking about the neighborhood, but he was also talking about his little piece of it, a six-by-eighteen-foot curb-side patch of asphalt where his truck and all his belongings were parked. I had always known that people lived in their cars, of course, but I had never heard someone talk about "home" as the pick-up truck in which they lived. This Montavilla neighborhood was my parish, my patch of ground that would be covered by Brigid's mythical cloak. And so Mark, and all the other people living in their cars, in tents, and in doorways throughout Montavilla, would be my parishioners.

Clearly, not everyone saw people living outside as neighbors. A group of people in houses had begun meeting on Zoom to talk about "health and safety concerns" around the nearby Methodist church. Campers were not allowed on their property and this restriction was enforced by the church's janitor, but every inch of sidewalk around the church was covered with tents, many connected to each other with tarps.

I went to the first Zoom meeting of these so-called concerned neighbors.

"I just want everyone to be safe," said a middle-aged massage therapist whose business entrance was a few doors down from the encampment. "I worry about the hygiene issues. Feces in the bushes. Not good for anyone."

"We hate it," said a couple squashed together on their couch so they both fit into their computer's viewfinder. "We would move if we thought we could sell our house. But who wants to live across the street from that dump?"

"I've gotten to know some of them. I skateboard around in the evenings," said a young man named Jason who lived in a rental house right across from the biggest tents. "I am just so grateful to have a roof over my head. I think about what it must be like for those who don't."

Jason's compassion was drowned out by the complaints from the housed neighbors.

"We need a plan," said one of them.

"I wonder if you would consider inviting someone who is living on that block to come to your next meeting," I said as we were about to sign off.

"But there's nobody living on that block," said a representative from the local business association.

"I was thinking about someone living in a tent or in their car." I was thinking about Mark Love, who parked on the next block over from the church.

My suggestion was met with silence. The group resolved to write some letters to the city and help clean up some of the garbage that littered the sidewalks around the church.

My church's mission statement at the time was "Saints Peter & Paul celebrates the diversity of God's creation through joyful, prayerful worship, radical hospitality, and fellowship." In my experience, there wasn't much there to distinguish it from other church mission statements, which are all yawningly similar. But "radical hospitality" stood out and struck a chord with me and with anyone who knew the church. The phrase was the thread that connected the dwindling congregation with the other activities that happened in our space: Rahab's Sisters, Brigid's Table, an emergency "low-barrier" warming shelter, and a Crisis Kitchen which cooked and delivered free food to anyone who needed it.

While "radical hospitality" had appeared in Rahab's Sisters literature since 2003 and I'd seen it around before then, I was curious what it meant outside of church-land. I posed the question to a group of strangers on social media, asking what connotations they had with the term. Reading people's responses was like finding a much larger pile of gifts under the tree on Christmas morning:

> It makes me think about taking traditions associated with hospitality—gift-giving, party planning, cooking, host(ess)ing—and pointing them in the direction of, or using them in service of, justice and equity.
>
> The phrase makes me think of a couple of women I know who are simultaneously the most progressive/assertive/justice-minded people *and* really connected to their identities as Southern women and caregivers/nurturers.
>
> It's a Christian buzzword.

I just want to go to a low-key dinner party and not have some weird overdone drama created by the hostess... is it Martha Stewart on steroids?

My first thought was of opening one's home to people who are homeless.

It means a host with boundaries issues.

My associations lead me to think of self-abnegating (to a fault) efforts by women to accommodate others.

To me, it is a Christian phrase meaning to invite all to the table—fully inclusive Christianity.

Radical hospitality doesn't just ask "do you want to be with us?" It says, "how can we be with you?"

I immediately thought of my people-pleasing sister who goes overboard as a hostess.

It describes Abraham and Sarah's policy of welcoming the stranger.

Radical hospitality does have biblical roots: Abraham and Sarah and all of their descendants who were taught, over and over again, to welcome the stranger.

Rahab herself, after whom the church's Friday night ministry to women was named, provided hospitality in her own way. A woman described in scripture as a prostitute, she found her place in the survival industry. As the story goes, in the early 1400s, BC, she provided shelter to some spies, sent by Joshua to investigate the city of Jericho as a target for conquest by the people of Israel. Like many marginalized citizens of her day, Rahab lived in the city wall. City walls in ancient times were thick structures that doubled as apartment complexes, the city ramparts as roof decks suitable for entertaining and for sheltering foreigners not welcome in the city itself.

Rahab risked her life and reputation—such as it was—to help foreigners and protect them. Whether or not she did this willingly is a matter of some debate. But she made the strangers' safety equivalent to her own.

Welcoming, feeding, and sheltering strangers and foreigners is a theme throughout the Bible, especially in stories told about Jesus by the evangelist Luke. Of all the biographers of Jesus, Luke's stories most frequently highlight interactions Jesus had with the least, the last, and the lost. The traveling, trouble-making carpenter's son repeatedly puts his life and reputation—such as it was—on the line in order to protect strangers, outsiders, and social outcasts.

He makes friends with a tax-collector named Levi who invites him to dinner, along with a whole lot of other people who wouldn't be welcome in polite society: sex workers, people suffering from diseases that were thought to be a punishment for bad behavior, and Roman soldiers whom nobody liked. A dinner party with Jesus was kind of like a potluck with a group of people who haven't had access to a shower or laundry facilities for a long time combined with people from the wrong political party.

The word radical comes from *root* (like "radish," I was always taught). Jesus' Jewish roots would have taught him, like Rahab, to remember that his people were once strangers themselves, vulnerable and untouchable. The society he lived in was fragmented. Religion was not a narrow slice of some people's lives the way it is today, it was everything, and the religious structures of the day had lots of rules about who was "in" and who was "out."

Jesus had his work cut out for him. As someone on the move who didn't spend a lot of time in his own home, one of the ways that he practiced radical hospitality was to accept hospitality from others whose homes might not be considered worthy by the religious establishment. Tax collectors then were like drug dealers in our time: they made money off poor and desperate people at the expense of the health and safety of the rest of the community. They were associated with dishonesty and abuse of the working poor, yet Jesus regularly hung out with them.

In one story he invited himself to dinner with a guy named Zacchaeus, who was a rich tax collector and therefore considered by the religious establishment to be a sinner. Zacchaeus responds to Jesus by promising to give half of everything he has to the poor and making amends to anyone whom he has defrauded. Jesus' concern for the poor and his desire to relieve the rich of their wealth was contagious.

In another story, he welcomes a sex worker into the home of a Pharisee who would never have invited her himself. Not only that, but he allows her to give him a foot massage over dinner. When his host confronts him on this breach of decorum, he points out that the woman at his feet is actually providing better hospitality than the Pharisee.

The police came on a Tuesday night during Brigid's Table, while the needle exchange van was handing out supplies and encouragement to their long line of weekly regulars. Kevin was camped in the smoking section where he'd been for several days after my conversation with the police officer. I heard that it didn't go well, that the police were rough and rude with Kevin because he was Black. I didn't know that about him; I'd never seen

Kevin. I doubt I would have authorized the police to remove him from our property if I'd known. But the experience made me realize how complicated setting a table in the wilderness of that corner of Portland was going to be.

My responsibility was to keep congregation members safe, so they continued to feel good about feeding and clothing our parishioners who needed our support. Sometimes that meant kicking campers off the property. And at the same time, did I not also have a responsibility to protect our houseless neighbors from the police? And what about my desire to connect, myself, with the neighbors living in houses around the church? I needed to ask myself the question: *Who is my neighbor?*

Kevin moved over to the crowded campsite in front of the Methodist church. He showed up at the church from time to time for food and supplies; sometimes he just sat on the church's front step. It was a peaceful spot, especially in afternoon sun. I'm not sure he knew that I was the person who had told the police they could cite him for trespassing. One of the staff said it best in a text:

It all sucks and there's no great answers, and that makes me very sad all the time, but we help where we can.

Or, as Linda had written: *We can't do everything.*

A few months after first meeting Mark Love, I walked around the corner to explore the block where so many houseless people lived. It was a sunny afternoon in late September; the air was soft and warm, and it was the time of year when the sun began to sink noticeably earlier each day.

I passed a couple of burned-out cars right in front of the Methodist church. I had heard that they'd been set on fire a couple of nights earlier. Multiple stories about what had happened were passed around the neighborhood like a game of telephone.

I found Mark Love's truck a few blocks down from the church and the burned-out cars.

"I like to stay on the next block so I can keep my eye on everyone," he'd told me recently.

He was sitting on the tailgate of his pickup truck, dangling his legs and drinking a beer. A few feet away from him sat a forty-something woman with thick horn-rimmed glasses and a red bandanna that didn't quite cover dark roots under bright blond hair. She held a beer as well, and several empty cans on the sidewalk told me they'd been visiting for a while.

She saw me first and stopped talking. I could see her wondering: *who's this lady coming right towards us?*

"Hey, Sara, fancy meeting you here!" Mark said as soon as I came around his truck. I explained that I was in the neighborhood and thought I'd wander over to say hi.

"This is Renee." He gestured with his cigarette to his companion. "She's a local writer. If you ever want to know anything about Montavilla, she's the one to ask."

"Good to know!" I'd read a piece of hers in the neighborhood news. Knowing she was the kind of person who would join Mark for a beer on a Wednesday afternoon made her more than a byline.

"Want to sit? I've got another chair here somewhere." He pointed over his shoulder with his chin. The back of his pick-up was piled with miscellaneous household items under a tarp held down by rocks in each corner. No rope in sight, but it was obvious he wasn't going anywhere. A folded lawn chair's tattered webbing poked out from under one corner of the tarp. Without moving off the tailgate, he pulled back the tarp to reveal the chair in its threadbare, rusted entirety.

"There it is! Join us? I'm sorry I can't offer you a beer."

I said I'd join them another time. As I walked back to my church where I'd left my car and my to-do list, the sun low in the sky warmed my back. My spirit was warmed by the scene I'd just left.

Like Jesus and like the woman who bathes Jesus' feet, one didn't need a house or a particular position in society to practice hospitality.

Saint Benedict of Nursia, who founded a monastery outside Rome in the early 500s, is considered the Father of Western Monasticism. Benedict inculcated in his monks and all who followed a tradition of hospitality articulated in Chapter 53 of the monastic rule of his community: "Let all guests who arrive be received like Christ." In other words, those who strived to be good followers of Jesus and good monks were encouraged to treat guests with the same care, reverence, and eager anticipation that you might treat Jesus if he showed up unannounced.

Benedict also suggested that "in the salutation of all guests, whether arriving or departing, let all humility be shown." The Benedictine way of radical hospitality includes physical acts of welcome and farewell to accompany words. We don't think much about acts of hospitality in our culture. Perhaps shaking hands is the closest we come to it, and during the pandemic, this wasn't happening. Some of us began to offer a small bow of the head or shoulders instead. In other parts of the world, such bowing to one another is customary when they greet guests or enter or leave someone's home. In the time and place where Benedict wrote, this was not the norm. For Benedict, welcoming all as Christ was honoring people who did not expect such honor, as if they were royalty. As if they were, in fact, God.

What I saw in what was happening in my new little church on 82nd Avenue was radical hospitality, hospitality that had long been part of the community's identity. I was watching it shift into a pandemic version of itself. If radical hospitality always meant welcoming people at the door with no strings attached, radical hospitality in a pandemic meant going out and looking for people who needed food or soap or masks. If radical hospitality always meant welcoming women from all circumstances to the church on Friday nights for Rahab's Sisters, now a mainstay in the community, in a pandemic it meant welcoming men, as well. Hospitality during the pandemic meant the end of an era. As much as "by women, for women" had been part of Rahab's Sisters identity since its inception, radical hospitality could no longer be limited to vulnerable women. Like Brigid's Table on Tuesday nights, Rahab's Sisters would be welcoming Kevin, who, even after he moved over to the encampment in front of the church around the corner, hung out on our steps where he felt safe.

Chapter 6

All the Marys

O ne afternoon in July, a few months into the pandemic, Anneliese, the director of Rahab's Sisters, asked about the extremely Anglo Mary statue at the back of the church. From behind a mask, she said, "What's up with that Virgin statue? The one with the kneeling bench?"

The particular version of Mary to which she referred sat like a queen in flowing blue and red robes, crown on her head and babe in her lap reaching for the lily in her hand. In front of the statue is one of those prayer bench votive-stands that often invites even the most irreverent agnostics to take a knee and light a candle for someone they love.

"That's Our Lady of Walsingham," I said, thinking to myself that Anneliese, while never irreverent, was probably agnostic, at least when it came to Mary. Most of the current volunteers and staff of Rahab's Sisters reflected the dominant religious soup of inner Southeast Portland and ranged in theological perspective along a short continuum from agnostic to atheist.

"Why do you ask?" I wondered aloud.

"I was sitting in the sanctuary opening the mail"—a normal COVID-19 practice done to avoid taking up air space in the small parish office where the mail arrived—"and I looked up at the statue while opening the last envelope and out came a twenty-thousand-dollar check! Maybe I'll tell this story in our next newsletter."

If the power dynamic in the church was traditionally patriarchal despite the many women upon whose work the church depended, Saints Peter and Paul Episcopal Church's saintly lineage was a little different. The parish followed the common, although not universal, Christian practice of naming itself after saints. Saint Peter, one of Jesus' first disciples, starts out lovably dense in every Bible story in which he's given a speaking part. It is Peter who, when under stress, forgets himself and denies any association with Jesus. Despite this gross lapse in loyalty, it was to Peter that Jesus promised the keys to the kingdom, rewarding his earthy, at times flaky, eagerness to follow. Statues and icons of Peter often show the saint holding keys.

Paul, the Bible's most prolific letter-writer and the person sent out to convert the non-Jewish world, was opposite from Peter in every way: he was educated, self-absorbed, neurotic, and confused about women. He is usually depicted with an early Mediterranean version of pen and paper. When Peter and Paul appear together, they often hold a model church between them. In the worship space of the church named for Peter and Paul, they are pictured in several paintings as grizzled old white men, their heads close together, faces cheek to cheek, as if to say *See, we are as different as we can be and yet, here we are.*

But Peter and Paul were not the only saints whose images graced the church. Mary, that most multi-faceted of saints, dominated the sanctuary.

I was delighted by the idea that Our Lady of Walsingham cared enough about sex workers and the sexually vulnerable to send Rahab's Sisters twenty thousand dollars. But this miracle sounded like the kind of thing I might read about on a conservative Catholic website, not a bi-monthly newsletter intended to inspire donors of all faiths and no faith. Although she never did write the newsletter article about opening the check in front of Our Lady of Walsingham, my conversation with Anneliese prompted me to learn more.

In a disintegrating cardboard file box of papers in the church office I found a stack of mottled photocopies telling the story of the statue of Our Lady of Walsingham. When the current church was built in 1960, the statue was added as a small side chapel just inside what used to be the main entrance. Parishioners regularly referred to the small altar, statue, and candle stand as "the Walsingham Shrine."

The ladies—I'm sure they were ladies—who prepared the leaflet I discovered had done their homework, and written not just the history of the Walsingham Shrine at Saints Peter & Paul but also the history of its namesake. It seemed that at the time that Our Lady made her appearance in

Walsingham, England in 1061, she was a bit of a troublemaker, wanting to remind the locals that Jesus was everywhere, not just in Jerusalem. Mary's command to those who saw her was to construct a pilgrimage site that would be a replica of the original place in Nazareth where Mary heard the word from Gabriel that she was to bear the Son of God.

I learned that the original shrine and monastery built in her honor were destroyed during the wave of anti-Romanism that characterized the English reformation. In the 1800s, Roman Catholics began visiting the Walsingham pilgrimage site as their own reminder that their favorite saint could be found in England as well as Rome. Anglicans, from whence my little church descended, were reluctant to cede Mary to the Romans and so rebuilt their shrine as a pilgrimage site and retreat center.

In the context of the little town of Walsingham, the shrine to Our Lady was subversive, a root of Roman Catholicism not necessarily welcome in post-reformation England. I appreciated that subversiveness, a reminder that Christianity is not uniform and tidy, especially not my chosen Christian pathway of Anglicanism. Even today, there is something subversive about Mary among Episcopalians: some give her a central place in our faith and practice, and others don't. But regardless of her place in the hearts of various Christians, few deny that she has been a source of particular comfort and inspiration to the poor over twenty centuries.

In Southeast Portland, the Our Lady of Walsingham shrine at Saints Peter & Paul became the locus of a weekly intercessory prayer group that lasted at least fifty years, ending when the last member of what was called the "Walsingham cell" moved on in the early 2000s.

Even though I arrived almost twenty years after the Walsingham cell group disbanded, and despite the dust and neglect surrounding the shrine, I felt a residual holiness. From her position in the back of the church Mary, with her covered head and elegantly draped robes, had a view of everyone who came and went between the sanctuary and the rest of the church building. The sanctuary was empty much of 2020, while the rest of the building became a busy hub of mutual aid and radical hospitality. It always seemed to me that Mary approved; I was glad to think she was as connected to the sex workers and houseless people who relied upon the church as she was to generations of proper English pilgrims or the prayer group that gathered around her statue in years past.

Our Lady of Walsingham was the first Mary one encountered when entering the sanctuary, but she was not the only one and by no means the most prominent. Around 2010, Our Lady of Guadalupe, patron saint of Mexico, joined Mary of Walsingham.

The small congregation of Saints Peter & Paul includes an even smaller community of Spanish-speaking Episcopalians—most former Roman Catholics—who, in pre-COVID times, held a Misa, or mass, every Sunday at noon. For the past several years they were led by Karen, an Anglo priest with impeccable Spanish who was on salary for six hours each week. Those of us from the English-speaking portion of the congregation referred to this part of our community simply as "the Misa community" or "Misa folk."

For the Misa community, church was not church without at least one image of the Virgin of Guadalupe.

Like Mary of Walsingham, the Virgin of Guadalupe had the familiar look of Mary everywhere: calm and serene, motherly and divine. Stars sparkled from her blue-green cloak, and light emanated from her as though a golden spotlight sat on the ground behind her aimed at her back and shoulders which were broader on Guadalupe than on many other manifestations of Mary. There are two Guadalupes at Saints Peter & Paul: a heavily shellacked painting next to the piano with its own prayer candle stand, and a beaded tapestry near the altar flanked year-round with tiny white Christmas lights which were as much of a fixture in the space as the tapestry itself. Those Christmas lights made me feel right at home at that church from the start.

The Virgin of Guadalupe was herself a bit of a troublemaker.

When I traveled to Mexico City in 2014, I learned the story of the beautiful brown woman who appeared to Juan Diego, an indigenous Mexican peasant, in 1531. She appeared several times over several days, each time with a message: *Please tell the archbishop about me and ask him to build a church in my honor.* Juan Diego went to the archbishop after each appearance; each time the archbishop refused to believe him. Three or four miracles later, the archbishop finally believed Juan Diego and believed the Virgin. One can only imagine what the archbishop, who would have been Spanish, thought of this indigenous-looking brown Virgin telling him what to do.

Our Lady of Guadalupe was the ultimate syncretistic saint, speaking in the native language and appearing to many of the locals to be a somewhat Christian-looking version of the Aztec earth-mother goddess Tonantzin. Hers was the first indigenous expression of Christianity the diverse peoples of the region we know as Mexico would have seen. She represented the integration of the colonial Christianity of the Conquistadors, in residence in Mexico at that point for only twelve years, and the native religion of the Aztecs.

Mary's appearance, on the little hill of Tepeyac five centuries ago, the story of her persuasion of the archbishop, and her enduring presence throughout their messy history is a ubiquitous reminder to her people: *whatever they do to you, don't ever forget that this is your country. You are more than simply people who have been conquered and oppressed. You are my people.*

During the pandemic, all but one or two Misa folk were unable or unwilling to connect to one another with Zoom, either because they did not have computers or because of prohibitive work schedules, or simply because church outside of an in-person mass made no sense to them.

In the years before COVID-19, the Misa community had a huge celebration each year that began at midnight on December 11 and stretched into the early hours of December 12, celebrating *las mañanitas.* Named for a traditional birthday song sung in the first hours of a birthday, *las mañanitas* celebrates the Virgin of Guadalupe beginning before dawn. In 2020, the small handful of women who met regularly with Karen either on Zoom or by phone explained to her that *las mañanitas* was very important to celebrate, no matter what.

My 2014 visit to Mexico had been in December and so I was acquainted with the celebrations that took place there in honor of their patron saint. I'd been on retreat with a group of people from Portland learning about liberation theology alongside Mexican history and culture. On December 11 we took a long bumpy drive in our crowded van from Cuernavaca to Mexico City, about fifty miles along a road full of thousands of pilgrims making their way to the basilica, a pilgrimage site for millions every year. They flocked to the city in packed pick-up trucks and in cars full of children, Guadalupe banners, and picnic baskets. Many traveled miles on foot, carrying paintings of the Virgin on their backs.

When we arrived in the city and settled into the large drafty convent where our group was staying, we walked, with hundreds of thousands of others, several long blocks to the basilica. The wide pedestrian streets along the way were filled with vendors selling souvenirs. I managed to find a fleece jacket, which was a good thing, as it was chilly after dark in Mexico City in December.

The square in front of the basilica was full of traditional Aztec dancers who gathered together from all regions of the country for this annual celebration. The rhythmic power of their drums and movement reminded me that Our Lady of Guadalupe was not and would never be a European import but sprang from the heart of Mexico, from the earth mother herself.

In December 2020 at Saints Peter & Paul, this celebration looked very different.

When Karen initially shared the service bulletin with songs and prayers, I balked.

"That's a lot of music for our musician to learn. A lot of songs for one service." There were about nine songs; more than would normally occur in one of our worship services. Our musician, Val, was a talented singer taking a COVID-gap year from a prestigious conducting program on the East Coast. *I don't really sing in Spanish*, she had told me recently, after learning a Spanish song and singing it beautifully. *My languages are French, Latin, Italian, and German.*

Karen went back and spoke with Rosa, who was the primary advocate for the service.

"The songs are all very important," Karen said.

"I wonder if we could just sing one or two verses of each?"

I realized as I asked this that I was more concerned for the flow of the worship (nine songs!) than I was for the Guadalupe celebration. I quickly relented.

After much back-and-forth about how to offer the celebration in the sanctuary in a COVID-safe way, live-streamed on Zoom so that people could participate at home, we gathered on a Saturday morning: Karen, me, my son Nathan to hold the camera, Val, a couple of other people to sing along, and another parishioner on guitar. Everyone stood six feet apart and my son was responsible for shifting the camera back and forth from the large, beaded tapestry of Guadalupe to the musicians. The tapestry had been draped with crepe garlands and surrounded by buckets of red and white roses, some real, some silk.

My part was simply to say the opening words: "Bienvenidos a la Iglesia Episcopal San Pedro y San Pablo. Gracias por estar aquí con nosotros."

(*Welcome to Saints Peter & Paul Episcopal Church. Thank you for being here with us.*) My presence and these simple words into the camera were a way to connect me to our small Spanish-speaking community which was both dispersed and central to the identity of the parish.

Karen then explained, as we did every Sunday morning, the importance of muting oneself to sing along to the music because of Zoom audio delays. There were about eight people on the zoom screen, four from the Misa, all women, and four from our English-speaking community. The Spanish-speaking women did not mute themselves and sang each song as loudly as they could. Their ability to participate in this way with these songs that had deep meaning for them was far more important than the aesthetics of "best practices" for church music on Zoom.

After my words of welcome, I sat with my laptop in a front pew out of the camera's sight. I watched the faces of the women singing their traditional songs on Zoom, their voices slightly off key in addition to being out of sync with one another and with the piano a few yards away from where I sat. In my mind's eye was another video pane of Aztec dancers with their drums and cowrie shells singing the same songs on the plaza of the basilica in Mexico City.

We were a long way from that celebration in every way, and yet borne out in our small, odd, COVID celebration of Las Mañanitas was everything the Virgin of Guadalupe stood for: the triumph of local, indigenous tradition and identity over some imported, colonial style of worship. In this triumph she stood for liberation through holding on to identity, rather than giving over to some "norm." The Virgin of Guadalupe essentially said to the indigenous people of Mexico: *you are who you are, you are people of this land, and I am with you. I am one of you.* She was radical, no-strings-attached hospitality for a whole nation. No wonder our parishioners of Mexican descent loved her so much. She was not trying to make them Spanish or even to make them Catholic. She was not trying to change them.

Almost every time I gave a presentation to a church or community group about Rahab's Sisters, someone would ask:

"So how does this program help to change these women, or at least their circumstances?"

I had not yet come to know Our Lady of Guadalupe when Rahab's Sisters started; it might have helped if I had.

One Sunday afternoon in 2008 I stood in front of such a group, a sheaf of fliers on the lectern in front of me. I'd learned long ago never to hand something out until after I was finished speaking. I'd just finished talking about a typical Friday night, the range of women who came through our doors, and how people could support us through donations, cooking a monthly meal onsite, or sponsoring a sock drive.

"I'd love to answer any questions," I concluded.

"What do you do to help them?" asked a man in the front row. There it was. I had just described everything we did, so I knew he was asking something else. He steadied a foam cup of cold coffee on his knee.

"What do you mean, exactly?"

"I mean, do you get them to change their lives? Do you get them off the streets?"

"Not all the women we serve are *on* the streets. They come from all walks of life. What they all seem to have in common is how much they enjoy being with other women in a warm, dry place for an evening when no one is asking anything of them."

"But what about the prostitutes? Aren't they supposed to repent?"

Hoo, boy, I thought.

"We're all supposed to repent, right?"

A couple people chuckled, for which I thanked whichever Mary might have been looking down at me at the time.

"What we offer," I continued, "Is a quality of interaction—a quality of relationship—that we hope will make women see themselves as we see them. That's all we can do."

I hadn't always understood that just *seeing* someone was what I could offer to the most vulnerable, hurting people I met. Before hosting Rahab's Sisters Friday after Friday, I thought everyone in need wanted to be fixed, like a car or a broken appliance.

In East London in 2002, a girl named Mary had been sleeping under some bushes in a churchyard on Whitechapel Road, a few blocks from where Jack the Ripper had done his work. She was about sixteen, but the lines around her eyes and around her mouth made her look sixty. She carried her belongings in a dirty pillowcase, and she wasn't allowed in any of the local shelters because she had lice. Father Brian told me she was probably hiding from her pimp, her stepfather, her dealer, and the police. The weather was expected to turn any day.

Brian took her for curry one afternoon and asked her what she needed. "Just a few bob." Five dollars. Maybe ten. Enough for a day's heroin. He wanted to find her a bed, a family, a job, a lifetime's worth of square meals and solid friendship. But right now, he wanted to get her a place where she could take a shower, get some clean clothes.

He gave her money and asked her to call the next day so he could gather some resources for her. I listened from the next room as he made a dozen phone calls, eventually finding leads for housing and even a job. Then he waited all that day and the next day for her call. She never called. A few days later, I was out again with Angela and Rayna in the Maze van and we saw her, stoned and waiting for a john. She wobbled on legs as thin as stilts. For all Rayna's big-heartedness, she didn't want to give Mary a ride anywhere because of the lice.

The next day, over another lunch at the local pub, I told Brian about seeing Mary. He leaned into our conversation, interested.

"She looked pretty bad," I told him, adding "I wonder whether she really wants help."

"Some people are like that," Brian said. He was silent for a moment, sipping the foam off the top of his pint. I wondered whether I sounded judgmental. I didn't mean to; I felt badly for him, that he did all that calling around on Mary's behalf and she never followed up.

While Brian drank his beer and we talked about other women I'd seen the night before—regulars he might know, as well as a few newcomers—I thought about people I had tried to help over the years. Eddie, a handsome, drunk ex-con; Susan, a heroin addict; Margie, who kept inviting loser guys home to live with her and her two children; and Donna, who was bipolar.

With them I had tried to help with a listening ear, advice, affection, or maybe a few dollars. But I saw then that it had always been about me. I wanted to be responsible for something good coming out of despair. I wanted to be someone who helped people and made a difference. I wanted to feel good about my own good works, and I wanted others to feel good about my good works too. All this trying to be good! Where was the grace in that?

Brian, Ken, Rayna, and Angela all showed me a different way of connecting with people who needed help, without trying to change them or trying to elicit a particularly grateful response.

Brian wanted to talk some more about Mary. "She's like the Blessed Mother."

"What do you mean?" I had been wanting to ask about that other Mary, the Blessed Mother.

"Our Lady was a teenager with no education, nothing special about her, and yet God adored her, picked her out of a crowd. Out of nowhere."

When he first said this, I thought he was being ironic, simply because this lice-ridden, rough sleeper was named Mary. I waited for him to continue, drawing finger-circles on the table with the water sweating off my glass.

"Who's to say this Mary isn't beloved in exactly the same way?" he said. "Or any of these girls? When I look at them, I see Our Lady." He was as serious as I'd ever seen him.

The other Mary—not the one sleeping under bushes, but Mary the Blessed Mother—was so much more present in the East End churches I visited than in churches where I'd worshipped in the United States. She stood larger than life alongside Jesus behind high altars or reigned on her own in Lady Chapels all over town. Plastic flowers and rosary beads lay at her feet wherever she stood, as she held out her arms in welcome. Arms of plastic, arms of stone, arms of porcelain. The ubiquity of Mary mitigated the cheesiness factor: she was important even if she was not always beautiful.

I had always associated Mary with Roman Catholicism. Growing up, all I knew about Catholicism were the Irish maids, many named Mary, who waited on my grandparents' generation, working behind the scenes six days a week in exchange for an attic room and a ride to mass twice a week. One of them, Mary Delaney, wore a "miraculous medal" around her neck, a nickel-sized oval disk of Our Lady with the words "I am a Catholic. In case of emergency, please call a priest" etched on the back.

"She's these girls," Brian was saying. "She's the Queen of Heaven but she could be any one of them. Young. Poor. Living in a rough time. Mother of God."

That night in 2002, back in the little room in Brian's house that I shared with Mark and Nathan, I propped myself up against the wall in the bottom bunk and opened my Bible to re-read the story of the first Mary. Mary, pregnant with Jesus, visits her cousin Elizabeth who is also miraculously pregnant, carrying a boy who will grow up to be John the Baptist. The two women—one presumes—are as happy to see each other as any two women sharing bonds of kinship and first-time expectant motherhood. Elizabeth, who is further along than Mary, feels her baby kick. The story goes that even the child in her womb is excited to see Mary. Mary responds, as many a devout Jewish girl before her had done, by giving God credit for the blessing of motherhood. *My soul proclaims the greatness of the Lord*, she sings. *My spirit rejoices in God my savior, for he has looked with favor on his lowly servant.*

I had heard choirs sing these words—called the "Magnificat"—at Westminster Abbey's grand evensong, and I had heard old ladies mumble them by twos and threes in small chapels during evening prayer. We sang them in the seminary chapel every weekday evening. I'd said them myself many times, but as I read them that night, the words took on new meaning.

From this day all generations shall call me blessed; the Almighty has done great things for me.

The Mary who says these words is simply a good Jewish girl praising God for the miracle of conception, as women had done before her and would continue to do after her.

I thought about the scrawny, lice-ridden Mary I'd seen under the streetlight the night before, hollowed-out eyes trying to focus on one spot so she wouldn't fall over. It was hard to imagine her expressing joyful expectancy about anything.

The Bible's Mary goes on to say, *God has cast down the mighty from their thrones, and has lifted up the lowly. He has filled the hungry with good things, and the rich he has sent away empty.*[1]

Then I understood that for Brian, it was the Blessed Mother Mary's voice saying "God has filled the hungry with good things" that he heard when he saw the other Mary. His care for her, and for girls like her, was not so that he could gain personal satisfaction from turning her life around, but because what it meant to him to be a priest was to do his best to see that the hungry were filled with good things. Never mind if the hungry kept turning tricks, shooting heroin, or stealing the silver from his church.

Brian wanted his Mary, the one who slept under bushes and never followed up on his offers of help, to experience the same surprise as the Bible's Mary, at being picked as a recipient of God's extravagance. I understood, finally, that feeding people or giving them handouts was not "enabling" (to use the language of the 1980s) or "ignoring root causes of poverty" (as people said in the 1990s). It was to surprise someone with the unlikelihood of attention and generosity. I knew, by this time, that my priestly work

---

1. There are as many different versions of the Song of Mary (Luke 1:46–55) as there are translations of the Bible. In this book I have used the version from the Book of Common Prayer (1979) of the Episcopal Church, itself descended from the Elizabethan King James Bible (also known as "the authorized version").

would be bound up with Mary of the Magnificat and this young Mary of Whitechapel Road.

It made a difference to me to understand both Marys a little better. I began to see the Bible's Mary, not as Mary with the blue dress and the halo, revered by those Christian denominations that refused to ordain women, but as the young girl who responded to her own unplanned pregnancy by singing the Magnificat, singing of God's reversal of her fortunes and the fortunes of all the poor and marginalized. The song was a rallying cry for anyone who wanted to do good in her honor. Surprise people. Confound their expectations.

I found myself thinking about Mary a lot that summer in the East End. I began to see her in the young women who came out of the shadows for a sandwich and a pack of condoms when I was out with the Maze Project. I saw her in the South Asian women who sat on sidewalks in London's more heavily touristed area with an infant on their laps, begging for spare change and food.

One day while visiting Ken Leech at St. Botolph's I picked up an anthology of essays and poems called *Mary: Mother of Socialism*. The book's contributors, including Ken, saw the Song of Mary, the Magnificat, as a Marxist manifesto. *Why not?* I thought as I read it. If Mary was the mother of all things—as some of my seminary classmates were fond of saying—why not the mother of socialism? Why not a voice for transformation of the whole world order?

From Mary, the simple peasant girl who could have been as poor and desperate as any of the girls I met on the streets in East London, I could imagine Mary, the mother of my own doubt and selfishness, Mary, the mother of my own hope, my own fledgling desire to make a difference in people's lives by surprising them with God's generosity.

This Mary, whom I came to understand in East London in 2002, I called "Mary of the Magnificat," or "Mary of Nazareth." She was the same Mary that Roman Catholic pilgrims worshiped in Walsingham and catholic-leaning Anglicans worshiped at my little parish in Portland. She was the same Mary who appeared in 1530 to Juan Diego in Tepeyac, Mexico, whose image millions of pilgrims carried from all over Mexico to Mexico City every December 12th.

I attended an ordination service with Brian in that summer I spent in East London. The person being ordained, a young man named Bradley, had been an intern Brian supervised a few years earlier. We took a train to a London suburb; it was rush hour and we stood most of the way. Brian was to be the preacher at the service and was quieter than usual while the train jostled us from side to side. At one point, he apologized.

"I figure I better think about what I'm going to say."

I wanted to be that kind of preacher who could talk without any notes, but I didn't think I ever would be.

We walked a few blocks uphill to the church, where I enjoyed several minutes to myself as Brian prepared for the service. We were quite early, and I sat in the dimly lit sanctuary alone, listening to the sounds in the adjoining hall of church folk preparing for the reception afterwards. In another room, the choir rehearsed an anthem. The sanctuary was simpler than many I'd seen in London, with modest granite columns and white-washed walls. A ten-foot statue of Mary stood in an alcove to the right of the altar, close to where I sat. Mary looked out at the empty pews and at me, her head slightly lowered, in modesty or curiosity, I wasn't sure which. But there was something querulous in her stance. *Do you really understand all this?* she might have been about to ask.

Did I understand it? I was beginning to get that although millions of people claimed to be followers of Jesus, by virtue of calling themselves Christian, it was very hard to *actually* follow Jesus. I wanted to be the kind of follower who had something to do with the changes Mary sang about: the hungry fed, the powerful toppled. I was beginning to see that this might even be part of a priest's job, to remember that God turns things upside down, and sometimes even to be the person to do the turning. This took shape in my mind very vaguely, but I shared it with Mary anyway. *This is the kind of priest I want to be.* She was right there, looking down at me after all. This was my first conversation with Mary. I was coming to her rather late in life without much to show for myself in the Marian devotion department; she welcomed me, nonetheless. Radical hospitality.

In 2017 I visited, along with hundreds of others on a cold sunny day in January, the Church of the Annunciation in Nazareth, Mary's hometown. The Church of the Annunciation is an enormous structure built in the 1960s, and like so many churches in the middle east, built on top of an older church which was built on top of a still older church, churches all the way down to the spot which is believed to be the spot where Mary lived with her family and where the Angel Gabriel interrupted her spinning one day—or her reading, depending on which iconographer you believe—to tell her she was to be the Mother of God.

The modern church, as large as any medieval cathedral, features dozens of enormous icons of Mary, many made from ceramic tiles, given to the church by Catholic peoples from all over the globe. There was a Guadalupe from Mexico that did not look like the paintings of Guadalupe I was used to seeing; this showed a young woman with wavy Charlie's Angels hair and lots of pink and lime green colors woven through the background. The United States contribution was a modern collage of pieces of aluminum at odd angles. Mary looked like she was wearing a haute couture coat of scrap metal. Other icons were more traditional, featuring a renaissance-era Madonna and child or Mary looking up at Gabriel with that combination of marvel and acceptance that only Mary could pull off.

All of these Marys were the same Mary as that ten-foot stone Mary in the suburban church outside of London where I had my first real conversation with her. She, in turn, was the same Mary whose woodcut image appeared on a t-shirt I found online in 2020, Mary with her fist raised in the air, encircled by the words: *Fill the hungry, lift the lowly, cast down the mighty, send the rich away.*

"You better think twice about wearing that t-shirt," said my husband Mark when I unwrapped it. "We're the rich, you know."

He was right. We were not rich in the sense that I always thought of rich people when I was a child, people with servants, circular driveways and limousines. But we lived in a cozy house where we never had to worry about paying for heat or hot water, we put our son through college debt-free, had fully funded our retirement by the time we were sixty, and regularly donated modest sums to our church and numerous organizations. We were secure in every way. We were rich.

And yet I was in love with Jesus who told people like me to give it all away to the poor. I embraced Mary's Magnificat as my own credo. Over decades this tension was with me like a tangled hank of yarn I wanted to use to knit something beautiful but which I could never untangle. The closest I got were lines of sermons that came to me in the dark early hours of Sundays in late 2020:

We view the promises to the poor in the Magnificat through the lens of a zero-sum game. In God's economy, it's not a zero-sum game.

Good news for the poor is good news for everybody.

The gift to the rich is the gift of detachment. Letting go of the power of possessions.

For those who are rich, Jesus takes away our illusion that we are supposed to have power over the poor . . .

This was not a tension I would resolve in one sermon or perhaps even in one lifetime. And I wasn't sure resolution was even the point.

I did, however, keep trying to surprise people with extravagance. I met a couple on a Friday night at Rahab's Sisters named Heather and Mitch. Minus the pregnancy, they could have been Mary and Joseph looking for room at the inn. We gave them food and blankets to line their damp tent a few blocks east of the church. Heather was looking for a pair of winter boots that fit her; none from our meager supply did.

"I wear an eight. No, a seven. No, maybe an eight," she was saying, a new knitted hat pushing her thick bangs over her eyes.

"Show her the bottoms," Mitch said, his voice kind.

She put one hand on his shoulder and used the other to pull her ankle up so I could see several quarter-sized holes in the bottom of her shoes, calluses showing through. It was October and the rains were coming.

I heard someone say that Mitch stood at a nearby intersection most of each day holding a sign asking for money. *Signing*, everyone called it, treating it like a nine-to-five job. I bought a pair of size eight lined boots and three pairs of thick socks and found Mitch signing the next day. The light changed before I could slow down and hand him the bag so I drove around the block and hoped for better luck.

At first, he didn't remember me.

"These are for Heather," I said.

His face, leathered beyond his thirty-something years, broke into smile lines.

"Wow, thank you. Thank you."

I drove home to my cozy house not pleased with myself but with a nagging sense of anxiety. I wanted to find a way to get boots for all the Heathers of the world, or at least my corner of it. For that, I was going to need help from all the Marys.

One afternoon, later in October, I dusted off the altar on which the statue of Our Lady of Walsingham sat, shook out the linen that lay at her feet, scattering dust and matchsticks, and smoothed it with my palms. I lit a couple of candles, one for everyone suffering from COVID-19 and all of its uncertainty, and one for the congregation. Kneeling on the hard shelf of the candle stand, I knew that Mary had been a comfort to the people of the parish over the years, and I hoped that I could be, also. I also hoped that both of the Marys at my little church, and all the Marys, would embolden me in the work of radical hospitality.

Chapter 7

Lessons from Rahab

"If I can give it to you, I will. If I can't, that sucks."

—ANNELIESE DAVIS

One night in 2004, early on in the life of Rahab's Sisters, Carol and I walked along 82nd looking for women to invite to the church. Carol had been with Rahab's Sisters from the very beginning. She taught the rest of us to pray for open eyes as we met women on the street and at the church door. Back then she still dyed her hair, although I'm not sure when, because every time I saw her she had a bright white stripe an inch or two wide across the top of her scalp like a skunk, with a shiny dark brown bob hanging on either side of her heart-shaped face.

A large old Buick, dark blue or black in that light, pulled up down the block, barely stopping to let a woman out in front of a convenience store, and then it drove away in a hurry. The woman, with long wavy hair and thick bangs, wore strappy sandals and fishnet stockings on that rainy December night. She went into a phone booth—still ubiquitous on 82nd back then—where thirty minutes earlier Carol and I had left one of our pink quarter-sheet fliers. *Rahab's Sisters: no-strings-attached hospitality in the church with its light on.*

I wore a purple raincoat over a fleece pullover over a clergy shirt tucked into jeans. The rain had poured off the bottom of the jacket to make a sopping wet band across my jeans. My sneakers were soaked through, and

I was glad I had put on wool socks. Ever practical, Carol wore a long rain-coat and wide-brimmed hat with rubber boots. We'd walked for an hour, covering the length of 82nd in both directions, chatting as we went. Our aim was to distribute fliers in phone booths and bus shelters, and to invite any women we saw to stop by the church. But the rain was coming at us sideways and not many people were out on foot. We had nothing to offer the cars that sped by.

"You know," said Carol, lunging to avoid a puddle, "I wonder about some kind of focus group."

"What do you mean?" She worked for the county in an office that did things like focus groups; I worked for a church which did not.

"It would be great to gather some women together who could tell us how we could support them."

I knew Carol had a lot of experience doing this kind of thing—in her day job she worked with people on probation and parole and had spent a lot of time in and around jail—but I just couldn't picture it on 82nd Avenue. *Hi, you look like you're a sex worker. We are starting a new ministry at the church up the street. What would make you come in?* I guessed that was not what Carol had in mind, but it's what I pictured.

We hung back in the convenience store parking lot as the woman made her call, not wanting to cause trouble by delaying a scheduled check-in with her pimp. The flier was gone. Either someone had picked it up soon after we left it, or the woman in the phone both had pocketed it. Either way, it was a good sign.

"Hi there," I said, handing her another flier for good measure as she put down the phone. "We've got some hot soup, coffee, and condoms in the church up the street there." I knew that if I mentioned condoms, she'd know that our invitation was sincerely directed at her.

"*Flavored* condoms?" she asked, her face lighting up with hope.

I could tell by the way Carol's eyes widened just then that she was slightly thrown off by this question. I knew flavored condoms existed from my time with the Maze, but they seemed like a luxury in those early days of Rahab's Sisters.

"No, sorry."

"Aw, you gotta get the flavored ones." Up close, I could see that her heavy mascara was smeared into dark circles under her eyes, but that even darker circles spread out to her cheekbones under the mascara. Nonetheless, she was pretty energized when it came to condoms. "Anyone can get those cheap health department condoms!"

I quickly resolved to order a thousand flavored condoms. Over time, this exchange turned out to be my favorite story to tell potential donors, especially if they were women. "Think about it," I'd say, and pause. Asking them to imagine giving men oral sex throughout the day and night, I hoped they'd see that our offer of flavored condoms was a small, necessary grace, a second's sweetness in a hard life.

The woman said she might stop by later and wandered up the street, her large shoulder bag bouncing off her hip as she walked. I had a feeling we wouldn't see her again, and I was right.

Carol and I stood planted on the sidewalk, the glare from the 7-Eleven behind us haloing our shadows on the wet pavement. In those early weeks I wore my clericals: a white plastic collar attached to a black clerical shirt. A raindrop made its way down the back of my neck between the collar and my skin. Next time, I'd wear a turtleneck.

"Flavored condoms, huh?" Carol said, laughing. "I think we just had our focus group."

I was momentarily overcome by the feeling that the woman at the payphone—a young girl-woman, really—could have been me. A memory-cloud passed through my consciousness like a clip from a scary movie: 19-year-old me, a girl-woman late at night, underdressed and wearing ill-fitting shoes in the rain. It would not be the last time that a hazy memory from my own life would appear, uninvited, and fade just as quickly.

In Portland, there was a law on the books for years that women stopped by police in certain parts of town—including where Carol and I were walking—could not be found with more than three condoms on their person, because that would prove they had sex for a living. Our role was neither to break the law nor to enforce it, and so we put out condoms in a big bowl and let our guests take as many as they wanted.

There were a few used condoms in the gutter near where we stood. The door of the 7-Eleven behind us slammed open with its electronic security beep and I turned around to watch a man stumble out, loudly ruminating over a coffee refill. He threw down a cup, its contents splashing onto the ragged cuffs of his trousers. He paused to inspect the contents of the dumpster alongside the building before wandering into the dark of the alley. Even in the rain, I could smell the dumpster, overflowing with uneaten corn dogs and nachos. We heard the clink-clink of someone sifting through the recycle bin beyond the dumpster, looking for returnable bottles.

I turned back to the street in time to watch our girl get into another car about half a block away. Its taillights sparkled in the rain, tires searing the wet pavement as it took the nearest corner. A police car sped by in the opposite direction. Her advice about flavored condoms was perhaps our first, although not our last, lesson from Rahab.

The story of Rahab[1] in the Hebrew Bible is morally ambiguous. It takes place in a violent time, when no one could be trusted. Joshua, Moses' successor commissioned to decimate residents of the land the Israelites believed was given to them by God, sends some spies to scope out the city of Jericho. Rahab lived in the walls of the city, which in those days were large structures separating the community from the desert. It was not always clear from the story who was helping whom. Each depended on the other for survival. They spend the night with Rahab, and somehow the king of Jericho gets word that some Israelite spies have infiltrated the city walls. I've always wondered whether Rahab tipped off the king early on. Given the strategic location of her quarters, she may have been paid a steady retainer for such communication. The king knows what the spies are up to and asks her to turn them over to him. Instead, she sends the king's men out into the wilderness on a wild goose chase while the spies hide on her roof.

Later in the evening, when the city gates have been shut and the king's men are, presumably, still off searching for the two Israelites outside the city, Rahab sits down with her guests for a heart-to-heart. This part of the story is often read as Rahab's conversion: she decides to devote herself to the God of Israel from that day forward. However, one doesn't need to be a Hebrew scholar to see that Rahab the Harlot is also Rahab the strategic thinker. She explains to them why she has been protecting them. *I understand*, she says, *that the Lord your God is indeed God in heaven above and on earth below*. So. it seemed to her like a good idea to be on their side. And because her help for these men comes from very human, rather than divine motivation, she asks for something in return: *Since I have dealt kindly with you, swear to me by the Lord that you in turn will deal kindly with my family*.

Done, say the guys. *Our lives for yours*. If you protect us, we'll protect you, and everyone in your family.

We were not stingy about condoms or very much else in those days. Early on, we didn't have many guests. It took either extreme desperation

1. Joshua, Chapter 2.

or a great deal of trust to come off the street into a church, even if it was a neutral fellowship hall. Because we had few guests in the first few months, the guests we did have received lots of attention.

One night, a young woman came in with her bulky bag and skimpy coat and sat in a corner, as far as she could get from the kitchen, where half a dozen volunteers congregated with not enough to do.

"Hi, welcome." I went over to her after she'd sat down. "We've got spaghetti and meatballs, salad, brownies, and hot coffee. What can I get you?" I always loved offering people food.

She shook her head and didn't say anything.

"On that table over there we have underwear, condoms, some other hygiene products. Help yourself to whatever you need." She sat there. I had been through this before and was undaunted.

"Stay as long as you like. Make yourself at home." She met my eyes at this, and I saw just a hint of a glimmer of gratitude.

I went back to the kitchen and reported that for the moment, our newest guest didn't want anything to eat or drink.

"Maybe I'll talk to her," said Taryn. Taryn was on staff at the church and had been part of the first clergy group that opened Rahab's Sisters. Her smooth skin and bangs made her look younger than the 32-year-old mother of three that she was. This impression was amplified by her soft, high voice. People meeting Taryn for the first or second time were always surprised to learn that she had a master's degree in social work. She wandered over to our guest and sat down. A few minutes later she came back into the kitchen for a mug of coffee, a brownie, and a cup of herbal tea for herself. They sat for thirty minutes. Whenever I looked over at them, they were deep in conversation.

It didn't bother me that Taryn was able to connect with this young woman who said her name was Suzanne, and that I wasn't. For one thing, there was the issue of my collar, which I eventually decided was more of a deterrent to conversation than the invitation we clergy hoped it would be. For another, Taryn's young manner created trust with other young women who didn't necessarily want to talk with someone twice their age. Finally, I had no illusions about being all things to all people. My gifts lay in organization, starting new things, and bossing people around. Others were better at long, patient conversation, and I was grateful to them for that gift.

Suzanne looked beat up, literally and figuratively. She held one arm against her chest, as if in an invisible sling. Her face was framed by a messy pile of hair that sat on top of her head like a nest, the color of the black coffee she drank. Taryn came into the kitchen with two empty mugs and traded them in for a pile of clean dish towels.

"I'm just going to help Suzanne wash up," she said. She grabbed a bottle of dish soap. "I wish we had some real towels and real soap. We should stock those."

Our list of supplies grew according to the needs we learned about. One week someone came in asking for food for the little Pekinese she kept tucked inside her coat. We didn't have pet food, but we made sure to stock it after that. Another time, someone asked for the kind of hand sanitizer that can be used without water. We hadn't thought of it, but from that point on we bought purse-size bottles by the case, long before the pandemic made hand sanitizer a thing.

Suzanne was in the bathroom for a while, with Taryn waiting just outside the door. She looked a bit better when she came out. She'd brushed her long hair into a ponytail and taken off layers of clothes and was down to a white t-shirt and a pair of jeans Taryn had found for her on a table piled high with used clothing. Her arm was covered in a cloth bandage the size of a tissue, frayed to gauzy string at the edges with blood, now dried, seeping through the center.

"I really want to change that bandage," Taryn said to me when Suzanne was out of earshot. "We're not supposed to do that kind of thing, right?"

"If you're comfortable doing it, you should," I said. The church kept a well-stocked first aid kit in the kitchen. Taryn started to take out what she needed—alcohol swabs, gauze, tape, antibiotic ointment, scissors—and then simply pried the box from its wall bracket and took the whole thing over to the table in the other room where Suzanne sat.

Washed and bandaged, Suzanne was now ready for food, and I watched as Taryn brought her plate after refilled plate of pasta, meatballs, and more brownies. We all loved watching the women eat.

Suzanne stayed until the end of the night, and as we were cleaning up and getting ready to close up and send our security guard home, it became clear that she did not have anywhere to go. Again, Taryn came up to me when no one could hear and said, "I really want to make a little place for her to sleep out in the courtyard." We both knew she couldn't sleep inside. We said it was because of the alarm system, but in reality, it would be perfectly reasonable for Suzanne to take off with the silver. This would not go over well with the church board and could jeopardize Rahab's Sisters.

We found a dry, protected spot outside between the church hall and the church proper, and piled some more donated clothing and an old sleeping bag on top of some large pieces of cardboard we found in the recycle bin. Suzanne hugged Taryn when we all left. We agreed that we wouldn't tell anyone we'd let someone sleep on church property. When I asked Taryn, she said there was no sign of Suzanne the next morning.

Another lesson from Rahab: break all the rules. Or understand that there are no rules.

The original Rahab is definitely a rule-breaker in how she practices hospitality and helps strangers. She lets the spies from Joshua's army down by a rope out her window. On their way out, they tell her to gather her family together, and to tie a crimson cord in her window as a sign to the warriors to spare that house.

Rahab has been handed down through history as a model of a bad girl turned good, a heroine of the people of Israel. Every retelling of the story portrays Rahab as deeply spiritual, sacrificial, and faithful. But ambiguity abounds. Did she really perform a heroic act as an expression of her new-found faith, or did she simply want to save her own skin? Rahab's survival-driven resourcefulness, more than her presumed religious conversion, is what links her to vulnerable women of every generation. Rahab lived her life close to the edge, literally on the edge of the city. I have always believed that her human will to survive trumps big-picture questions of heroism or history. This was true for Rahab and it is true for her spiritual descendants.

I'd once met a Franciscan monk who ministered in the South Bronx. He said: "It takes about ten years for the people you're trying to serve to trust you." I felt about the evenings at Rahab's Sisters the way I did when I invited people to a party. We'd set up the space with candles, good food, and a ready supply of condoms (flavored) and sweets. We'd been there for two months, and some Fridays no one came in. Or three women would come in, or two, or four in the course of three hours. Sometimes they came in pairs, but usually alone. Some of them ate a lot, as though they hadn't had a good meal in weeks, circling their plate with their coat-clad arm. I wondered if they were used to people grabbing their food from them, or if volunteers at soup kitchens took their plates away before they were finished. Others were so happy for a place to sit down for good conversation that they just picked at their food while they talked. ·

On slow nights we walked the streets, always in pairs, inviting any women we saw into the church with its lights on. Cars zoomed by, their headlights glittering shafts of raindrops. One night, in the winter of 2004, it was Carol and JoAnne out on the street.

They walked past a bus stop at the edge of Montavilla Park—a dark, gaping hole in the nighttime streetscape—when a bus pulled up and a young woman got off. She was about fifteen and Carol said she looked so clean, with her clear skin and a straw-blond ponytail hanging down from her fleece ski hat, that they could tell right away that she wasn't from around there.

She looked around and asked them, "Do you know where Clackamas Town Center is?"

Clackamas Town Center is a shopping mall five miles south—the bus that dropped her off had been going north. She had either gotten on the wrong bus or stayed on the right bus far too long. It was about 9:30; the mall would have closed. She felt around for her wallet and realized she'd left it on the bus.

"Do you have a quarter so I could make a phone call?"

JoAnne invited her back to the church to use the telephone. As they walked the five blocks from the bus stop, the story came out in one-word answers. Like so many conversations with teenagers, it was like playing a game of twenty questions. She lived in a small town on the Oregon coast and was staying at her aunt's house. She and her cousins had been out with some friends, and she had mysteriously gotten separated from them. She wanted to get back to her aunt's house. All she knew was that her aunt lived near the mall. She had no idea where she was, where her cousins were, or how far away she was from her aunt's house.

Her story jogged my memory. I saw myself on another wet night long ago.

I sat curled up on the corner of a stranger's couch, making myself as small as I could, knees pulled up, shoes on the floor in front of me.

"Sorry I don't have anything to drink," said the guy, probably reading my mind.

"It's okay." In the light of his apartment without the disco ball or the whiny blare of the souped-up version of *Won't you stay a little bit longer?* in the background at the bar we'd just left, I had nothing to say. My mind was a blank. What was I doing there?

He was putting on some music. *If it's Marvin Gaye I should probably make a run for it,* I thought.

And there it was. I could name that tune in one note: the opening *wah wah* on the electric twelve-string guitar with pedal steel, and then the words: *I've been really tryin' baby* . . . .

That was enough for me. The rest is vague in my memory, but I probably said:

"I . . . I've got to go. Can you give me a ride home?"

"You just got here. We were just about to get comfy."

In a moment of clarity, I realized he and I were following different scripts. I had ridden home with him out of a vague curiosity that he might be more interesting than he appeared. He was setting the scene for a couch-to-bed session which was not the least bit interesting to me. I did not want to be his success story for the evening or worse, what he settled for.

"Never mind," I said. I got up, picked up my shoes and my coat and walked out into the rain, just like that.

I walked for what felt like miles. It was probably two o'clock in the morning. I felt rain seeping in through the sole of one of my shoes, and then the other. At one point I realized that the miles I'd walked were actually the perimeter of the apartment complex, and I'd made no progress at all. I finally got myself pointed in the right direction and headed north to the town.

I stopped at a breakfast place that would be open in a few hours. I was grateful to see a familiar landmark, even if it was one that showed me I was still three miles away from my own bed. When the place was open, there was always a line down its ramp, people leaning against the ramp's polyurethaned maple railings. I leaned against the railing for a moment, looking in from the outside, as I might have done even if the place was open. Home fries and bacon would have tasted good at that moment. I was hungry. And, I knew, even then, that I was lucky. An impulse toward self-preservation I might later associate with Rahab had propelled me out into the night and to a spot under those streetlights.

A car pulled up while I stood in the restaurant's outdoor spotlight looking lost, and some guys on their way home from a party brought me back to town. By that time, I was sober enough to know I probably shouldn't take a ride from them, but I just wanted to get home.

⊕

Though the girl Carol and JoAnn brought back to the church that night reminded me of myself in some ways, she was younger—high school, not college. She didn't seem drunk or high, just deer-in-headlights.

It was warm in the parish hall, and Carol's glasses steamed up as soon as the trio came in. I had begun to blow out candles and put away baskets of underwear, socks, and hygiene supplies. Other volunteers were tidying the kitchen, keeping the night's enchilada casserole warm in the oven just in case any latecomers dropped in. It was after 10:00—the girl had been riding the bus and trying to get to someplace familiar for two hours. She was shaky and more than a little confused when JoAnne and Carol brought her to the church.

She was younger than the other girls who usually came in on Friday nights, and she didn't have their hard look. I was used to seeing women with clouded faces that only barely hid a life of beatings, betrayal, and loss. This girl was not like them. She was out of place with her puffy white parka, which she eventually took off and clutched in her arms like a stuffed animal.

She sat down and we offered her something warm and dry to wear, something to eat, something to drink. She didn't say much, just shook her head. She had told us all she was going to tell us. She did seem to have one thing in common with some of the younger women we saw on Friday nights: no way was she going to let anyone be nice to her.

The older women who came in were different: they liked to tell their stories over and over again, and they were happy to take whatever we had to give be it soup, condoms, clothing, hats, or gloves. But the young ones, usually sent in by their boyfriends or dealers for a free meal or some condoms, hated to ask for anything.

"You sure you don't want some of this?" I asked, pointing to a steaming plate of enchilada casserole. "It just came out of the oven. I had some a little while ago. Mmm-mm!" I felt like an idiot as I kept talking to her the way I talked to my son when he was in preschool, but I really wanted the girl to eat something. It was the half-Jewish mother side of me leaking out.

There was so much we couldn't give the women and girls who came through on Friday nights: we couldn't give them back their childhoods, or a good education, or a safe place to live. We couldn't give them back their own children, whom many of them had lost. We *could* give them a hot meal, a hot drink, and a place to be with other women out of the rain.

She wasn't having any.

Unbidden, I wrapped a shawl over her skinny, shivering shoulders, a prayer shawl someone from a neighboring church had made from thick, marbled blue yarn. She pulled it tight around her. I'd given up on the casserole, but watching her shoulders relax just a little under the shawl gave me hope for getting her to drink a cup of hot cocoa. Carol was on the phone giving her aunt directions to the church from somewhere in Clackamas, and I heated some water. I mixed the cocoa with half-and-half, some cinnamon, and a few mini marshmallows. I put it down on the table in front of her.

"Take it."

No response.

"It'll warm you up, make you feel better."

Then she spoke for the first time since coming into the building: "I'll just wait for my aunt."

"Okay," I shrugged. I stopped short of saying, *Suit yourself.*

She reached for the cocoa and put her hands around the mug for warmth. She lifted the mug toward her mouth a few times but put it down without drinking. Finally, she got it close enough to blow on it, holding it near to her face to feel the cocoa's steam. After blowing on it a few times, she took a sip. Then another.

By the time her aunt arrived around 10:30, she had drunk the whole mug and some color had come back into her cheeks.

Her aunt was a large square woman with big hair and tennis shoes, clutching an old-lady handbag, although she didn't look much over 40. When she saw the girl, she burst into tears.

"Thank God, thank God. I called the police. I was about to call your mother. Thank God I didn't need to call your mother."

More tears were shed, hugs were exchanged, thanks were offered, and they went out into the night. The girl waved at us once over her shoulder, but her eyes were glued to her aunt and getting out of the church parking lot and away from 82nd Avenue.

Afterwards, I recounted the event to someone who had worked with women on the streets for a long time. *Another five minutes and she would've been in the back of a pimp's car, gone forever,* he'd said. *Lucky she ran into the right people instead of the wrong people.* He was right.

The lesson from Rahab on that night was not to worry much about the difference between dumb luck and divine intervention. Sometimes luck didn't have to mean something big. Or divine intervention could be small.

Another night, in early spring, a young woman walked along 82nd Avenue. She wore the kind of heavy, Michelin-man parka that I wore in the 1970s. Hers was navy blue, unzipped to the early spring air. She took big strides, with each step looking over one shoulder or the other. As she looked one way and then the other, the breeze held her long, wavy hair aloft. If she'd been a little older and a little skinnier, she could've been in a shampoo commercial.

My friend Margie—another volunteer—and I had practiced what I called our non-spiel:

Hey, how's your night going?

You okay?

Need anything?

We wanted to talk with any woman walking alone on 82 nd. If a woman we encountered stayed at all engaged in conversation, we'd hand her a goodie bag with a few condoms, some hard candies, and a quarter-sheet flier advertising our hospitality up the street.

It took us a while to catch up with the Michelin-man girl. She seemed to be sauntering in a casual way, but her legs were longer than ours. By the time we did catch up, we felt like the slightly-out-of-shape middle-aged matrons we probably looked like.

"Hey, how's your night going?" I asked.

"Pretty good. Just out walking."

Up close, I could tell she was on the street but not of it. Like the girl from the coast, she was clean, not just her hair and her skin but her clothes, her shoes, and her eyes, which made contact with mine, nothing to hide. I couldn't imagine she needed condoms, but I wanted to give her something. Our little goodie bag was all I had to give at that moment.

"Here's some condoms and a few other things," I said, handing her the bag. "We've got some hot soup and coffee up the street if you want to come hang out."

"Thanks. I'm good. Just out walking."

She was probably fifteen, maybe sixteen, school-aged, probably still living at home nearby in the slightly more upscale neighborhood on the hill leading to Mt. Tabor Park. We crossed the street, walked down to the next major intersection, and turned around. Across the street, she'd done the same thing and was walking in the opposite direction, leisurely on her long legs. Just walking and looking for something, I thought.

Would her parents want her walking up and down 82nd Avenue? Maybe she just lived with one parent. Maybe her mother's boyfriend had too much to drink, or maybe her mother was ignoring her. Maybe there was nothing to keep her there, and she wanted adventure. Or her older sister had left home with some guy and she wanted to find a guy too. Maybe she was bored. That's how she looked to me, bored and looking for something—probably without knowing what—on a Friday night on 82nd Avenue.

That's how it starts for some girls. Bored, lonely, going someplace where there might be some action, just going to check it out, with the safety of her own bed waiting at home. Stepping out for an evening daydream, a respite from a life of school, homework, acne, sports. Wondering what you could make happen, out on your own. That's what she looked like, and I was afraid for her, afraid the way I knew girls her age were rarely afraid for themselves.

I didn't ever see that girl again, but I felt as though I knew her; she was my younger self, walking a fine line between looking for trouble and staying out of trouble. And my grown self was walking a fine line between a friendly check-in and trying to jump in and save someone from a future that may or may not be waiting for her. If there was a lesson from Rahab here it was that sometimes a simple kindness—offering someone food and drink or just saying *hi* on the street—is the practice of hospitality. That night, it was the best that I could do.

Cathie's Lingerie & Novelties sat for decades at the end of a small strip mall at the intersection of 82nd and Powell Boulevard in Southeast Portland. The mall offered a microcosm of a particular urban landscape on the eastern edge of the city: a 7-Eleven, check-cashing/payday loan store, Western Union Office, Domino's Pizza, vacant storefronts, and Cathie's. Like most of the stores in the strip mall, Cathie's was open late. One Friday night in May 2005, Carol and I parked her van in the narrow parking lot, designed for a population that travels on foot.

We opened up the back of the van to offer hot coffee and goodie bags as women passed through the corner lot. Inside each bag was a card describing Rahab's Sisters:

On the streets? Need a bite to eat or a cup of hot cocoa? Want a warm, safe place for a few minutes? Take a break! Women of all faiths and women of no faith are invited to stop in.

A young girl—maybe fourteen—came out of a shadowy side street marked "Roadway Not Improved," wearing a tank top, sweatpants, and bedroom slippers.

"How are you? I asked. "Are you cold?"

"Just woke up," she answered as if that would suffice for both questions and wandered into the 7-Eleven.

Carol had always been curious about the lingerie store, and so we decided to close up the van to check it out, both of us shy about venturing in alone, out of place with our grey hair and expensive rain jackets. *So, this is where strippers get their clothes,* I realized as the bells over the door jingled behind us. There were eight-inch platform shoes in every color of the rainbow, and feather boas I'd dreamed of as a child—all kinds of things with feathers, mostly in pink and black.

The shoes reminded me of being in college and broke. I pored over the help wanted ads, desperate for cash with no skills to speak of. Every week, the same ad ran in the same column: *Dancers wanted. No experience necessary.* I loved to dance back then, and I thought maybe I could do that. But I couldn't see myself in those clothes, those shoes. Mostly the shoes.

Later, I learned that Cathie's held the record for Portland's largest collection of platform shoes, and it was the only sex shop on 82nd with an all-woman staff, catering to women.

"Are you Cathie?" Carol asked the woman with a thick blond ponytail and tinted contacts that made her eyes grass-green. She was tall and strong, at home in black tights and high black pumps. I'd heard about what good exercise pole-dancing was and wondered if that's where she got her muscular legs. The way she moved through the store and interacted with customers made me think she owned the place.

"Nope, there is no Cathie. That's just our name. I'm Lucy."

Carol began to tell her about the church up the street. As I went back out to the van to open up the tailgate in case anyone wanted coffee or conversation, I heard Lucy ask, "A church? I didn't know there was a church up there."

I opened up the van just as two women came out of the dark street, crossing the parking lot to the 7-Eleven, close enough for me to call to them, "Coffee?"

They came over, wobbling on shoes they could have bought at Cathie's.

"How's your night going?" I asked.

"Good," said the younger one.

"Tired," said the older one.

While they stood at the van, they traded lipstick and hand lotion with an intimacy that must have come from family ties or sharing a whole lot of life together. I figured it was both, and that they were mother and daughter. The older one's face was a lined version of the younger one.

I told them there were volunteers giving out hot soup, homemade cookies, new underwear, and flavored condoms at the church up the street, in case they wanted to stop in. The church was almost a mile north of Cathie's, a twenty-plus minute walk in those shoes.

"What kind of church is it?" asked the younger one, emptying packets of sugar into her coffee.

"Episcopal?" I said it with a question mark as I so often did, assuming they hadn't ever heard of us.

"Don't know that one."

I offered my standard follow-up line: "Kind of like Catholic, except with women priests, birth control, and no Pope."

"That's real nice. Maybe we'll stop by."

I heard that a lot. Most of the time, our invitation was not why they came; they came because someone they trusted from the street told them about us or brought them in. I watched the two women go into 7-Eleven and come out again—each with a Big Gulp—and turn the corner.

Carol came out of Cathie's Lingerie and told me she'd just had a long conversation with Lucy. She took a step closer, the lights from the strip mall shining on her heart-shaped face. "It was fascinating!" she said. Her eyes glittered with her particular inquisitive energy.

Carol had an uncanny ability to connect with people and make it look effortless. In a few minutes, she had managed to elicit Lucy's life story.

I grew up in a Church of God. In Kentucky, Lucy had said, when Carol told her about Rahab's Sisters.

I knew the type: a prefab building in a giant parking lot, with Wednesday night suppers and a reader board outside that proclaimed weekly choices between reward and damnation. One of those places set back from the road with its own baseball diamond and barbecue pit, with a huge kitchen where the women and girls cooked while the men discussed scripture and the boys battled in God's Little League. Everything in order and predictable, no questions asked about God, the universe, or anything. For women, certainty and submission.

Went to church camp every summer. Every summer the camp pastor took me into his office and put his hands all over me. All the time. Whenever.

"Did you ever tell anyone?" Carol would have asked.

Who would I tell? My girlfriends would be jealous. My dad would say I asked for it. My mom would say God was punishing me for something.

Carol had described her as being busy around the store while they talked, straightening packages of pantyhose, putting shoes back on their shelves, always working.

So, you know, I don't put a whole lotta stock in what they say, about goodness and all that. I don't go to church. Not this chick.

As I learned more about what draws women into the sex industry, I learned that most of them were abused as children, usually at home, sometimes at church, or at school. Sometimes you hear about a girl abused by another woman, but at church, the perpetrators are always men, taking unholy license. Lucy may have been one of the lucky ones. Who knows what else happened in her past before that night, but by the time we met her in her mid-20s, she'd survived enough to have gotten a job in this successful, women-oriented sex shop instead of being trapped by a pimp, living in the back of a car, or in and out of jail. I was struck by her straight-up posture, her clipped words, and her easy smile as she moved through the shop and engaged with customers. Everything about her said she was a strong person with some control over her own life. Like Rahab, she was her own woman. I wondered what made the difference. The lesson from Rahab was that survival and resilience comes from stepping out on one's own, breaking molds along the way.

I stood there in that parking lot in my jeans and New Balance sneakers, pouring bad church coffee from an insulated carafe into Styrofoam cups, looking into hollow eyes. I was sometimes accused of verbosity, but there I could not find the words to speak to the women in a way that bridged the gap between the safety of my life and the brittle edge of theirs. I was an outsider to their world and they were outsiders to mine.

But it didn't matter. Some nights I could only speak to them with coffee and homemade cookies, but I loved being there more than I loved being almost anywhere else. And it never ceased to be a marvel to me that I was there, a middle-aged mom in a minivan, and not inside with Lucy, shopping for platform shoes and sequined halter tops. Or looking in the window, hungry for some splash of bright wild color of my own.

Most of the women at Rahab's Sisters were downright hard to connect with. When Rahab started, we lit candles and put a tall votive in each of dozen windows in the fellowship hall of the church. Eventually members of the church board who worried about insurance liability asked us to switch to LED candles. The windows continued to throw a warm glow of welcome into the parking lot.

Within a few months, we needed a place to store the growing collection of supplies we gave away to women who came in. Through an act of great magnanimity and flexibility, the board of the church that hosted Rahab's Sisters suggested we convert the unused confessional box into a storage area. The church was one of the few Episcopal churches in the Pacific Northwest with a confession box, and it hadn't been used in decades. The confessional consisted of a pair of phone-booth-size closets side by side in a corridor that connected the worship space to the parish hall and kitchen. The wall between the two closets had a small window in it, with a sliding door across it. Just like in the movies. I loved that it was in the confession box that we stored all the flavored condoms and frilly underwear.

Some of the items were weekly reminders of basic needs the volunteers took for granted but which were coveted by women surviving on the street: toilet paper, laundry soap, shampoo, new underwear. Other items were tools of the trade: condoms, hand sanitizer, and makeup to cover bruises. No one wanted a woman who had been beaten. The amount of socks and gloves reminded us how much time they spent out in the cold. And that everything was disposable. We needed to teach that last lesson to well-meaning church women who knit hats and scarves for the women and then got hurt feelings when their handmade gifts were quickly lost or passed on. This, too, was a lesson from Rahab: sometimes you need to leave everything and everyone and run. When you stop, it's time for clean socks and underwear.

By the end of 2005, we were open every Friday and hosted twenty or thirty women each week. The growth had been slow but consistent. We didn't forget what the monk from the South Bronx had told us: *you keep showing up and they'll keep showing up*. Now most were regulars, although a few newcomers ventured in each Friday. They came in with their big bags and hollow eyes, many unable to look at me when I greeted them. Sometimes, they came in mother-and-daughter pairs. The mothers were more outgoing; the daughters quiet and sullen, perhaps no different from any other teen spending a Friday evening with their mom. Sometimes, women had children or grandchildren in tow. Usually, they came in alone.

"Hey, welcome," I said to a woman I'd seen once or twice before. I rarely remembered the names of the women who came in, despite my best efforts. In seminary we learned all the basic tricks: repeat someone's name as soon as you hear it, etch an associative word-picture in your mind, or introduce the person to someone else as soon as possible. None of it worked for me, especially with women whose names often changed from one week to the next.

This particular woman was named Wendy. She held a reusable grocery bag full of clothes and a tattered *People* magazine several weeks out of date. She was in her late 30s, maybe older, wearing a puffy coat that exaggerated her own puffy shape. "We've got roast chicken, vegetable soup, potato salad . . . what can I get you?"

Wendy sat down, clutching her bag. "I'm not hungry."

"Coffee?"

"Sure."

"Sugar?" I don't know why I bothered asking whether or not she wanted sugar. Like the women I met on the streets in East London, our guests always wanted sugar; lots of sugar.

"Mind if I sit down?" I asked when I came back with the coffee, a sugar shaker, and a spoon. She shrugged and pointed to an empty chair.

"How's your night going?" I asked, watching her pour spoonful after spoonful of sugar into her black coffee.

She shrugged again.

I resisted the urge to comment on the weather. I knew that someone who was warm and dry most of the time had no business talking about weather to someone who spent much of her time outside.

In seminary when we studied pastoral care, we learned to have conversations that included questions like *Where do you see God in all of this?* I suspected that a more seasoned priest might find a way to tease out that kind of information from Wendy, but I was reluctant to talk of God with someone who as likely as not had received abuse and neglect in the name of the church. Care meant something different to people like Wendy. Actions, not words, were needed. Perhaps the most I could do was to make her safe, warm, welcome, and well fed.

As she drank her coffee, she took off her puffy coat. She had a couple of layers on underneath. Many people who lived on the street wore their extra clothes instead of carrying them; if Wendy had a place she called home, it wasn't secure enough to leave her clothes.

"You sure I can't get you something to eat?" I asked, wiping my hands on an apron with "Hug An Episcopalian" stitched in white script over red canvas.

"You said you had soup?" Wendy asked.

"Yup. And garlic bread. Want some?"

She nodded and smiled. When I brought the soup, she moved her big bag from her lap to the floor. After the soup, she took off another layer, an oversized sweatshirt from a state college I'd never heard of, probably combed from the giveaway bin of a charity thrift store.

Like so many of the women I saw on Friday nights, Wendy didn't expect anything from me. Everything she got—a place to sit, a cup of hot coffee—was extra, a special grace. Even if she didn't ever thank us, I knew she got something from Rahab's Sisters that she couldn't get anywhere else. I loved bringing her plates of food. As I served her and watched her slowly shed layers of outerwear, a rush of satisfaction bordering on joy thrilled through me. When she left, she said, "See you next time." When she said that, I felt the same rush of satisfaction I felt when she ate the food I brought her, and something more. In being part of a place where women could come in from the night, lost or not, some piece of my own past was healing over.

Chapter 8

Hospitality on the Sidewalk

What were you getting yourself into, Mama?
when you brought me home
and told me you would protect me
although you didn't know how,
but you would find a way
because you always do.

—FROM "AN ADOPTED BOY WRITES A LETTER TO HIS MOTHERS"
BY NATHAN FAUST

T he Sunday after the death of George Floyd I was invited—along with hundreds of other clergy—to a gathering hosted by Black pastors. I'd come to the event with an unfillable pit of longing that hollowed my torso and made my teeth chatter. There were about two hundred people in the parking lot of a social service agency in North Portland, the historically Black part of town. We were mostly white, mostly masked. Other than rushed trips to the grocery store, many of us had not been around other people for months. There was Janice, whom I hadn't seen since moving back to Portland, a hospital chaplain who was delighted to escape her work and her children to come out for a few hours around her peers. There was Megan, one of my closest friends who hated being out and about during the pandemic. She leaned against a car apart from everyone else and left early. The president of the local ecumenical organization was there in her always-perfect bobbed hair and dark suit. I should have been happy to see friends and colleagues, but the pit gnawed at me.

A prominent Black pastor welcomed us and talked about the potential and the power of the current moment.

"And it is not *just* a moment, it is a movement!" His voice carried over the whole parking lot. "I want to invite anyone who wants to come forward and give us a word."

Open mics always fill me with dread. I'd been to too many events where someone took the mic and said too much for too long, derailing the purpose of whatever the occasion was. I find myself feeling mortified for the hosts at such times. At this gathering, the first person to speak was a white evangelical guy, pastor of a church I'd never heard of. He was big and blond, and took up a lot of space in the circle we made on the asphalt. No self-consciousness about being the first to speak, he embodied what some might call "toxic masculinity."

"Should we pray now?" he asked the crowd. "Of course we should! Pray with me, people. Bow your heads."

If you ever want to be sure I hold my head up high, just instruct me, in public, to bow my head.

"Heavenly Father, we just want to pray for peace. Peace in our hearts and in our city. Peace in the hearts of those who mourn right now. Peace in the hearts of people who protest, and peace in the hearts of the officers sworn to protect and serve. In the name of Holy Blood of Jesus. Amen?"

The crowd responded with a half-hearted, "Amen." He'd asked for too little, too soon, and too loudly. I scanned the edge of the crowd for Megan, hoping she hadn't already left. She was easy to pick out because of her height. I gave her a tiny shrug that I hoped would communicate "whatever."

A few more white people slipped easily into the empty circle as I waited for what I thought would fill the pit in my stomach and stop my teeth from chattering. I wanted to hear a Black voice of hope, a Black word of solidarity. I needed this hope and solidarity because of my son, Nathan, a tall, tender twenty-three-year-old whom we'd adopted at birth.

Early in the adoption process, the agency social worker explained that if we didn't want a Black or biracial child, we should be sure to specify that in our paperwork.

"No one wants to admit it, but most people are uncomfortable adopting transracially. So, if you're okay with a child who isn't white, be prepared that that's what you'll get."

We didn't hesitate; we would not exclude Black or brown from the ethnicity of the baby we were willing to adopt.

He was two days old when we brought him home. His birth mother was white, from an affluent family in Oregon's Willamette Valley. His birth father, who had grown up in Portland, was Black, and not part of Nathan's childhood.

We read voraciously and talked endlessly about raising a non-white child in America at the turn of the millennium. We knew that white Portland was not a great place to raise a Black child, but we were confident and hopeful that we could give our son enough love, security, and education to equip him for growing up in America. In the adoption system, Nathan being adopted by a Black family had always been highly unlikely; we knew that if we had not adopted him, another white couple in the adoption "pool" of families who could afford the adoption agency's fees would have.

We filled our bookshelves with children's books by Black authors. *Sam and the Tigers*, a powerful retelling of "Little Black Sambo," was a family favorite.[1] We put African ornaments on the Christmas tree, celebrated Kwanzaa, chose a Black friend as one of Nathan's godparents, and did our very best. I turned out to be a fierce mother bear of a mom and assumed I could protect Nathan from any harm that might befall him on my watch.

Neither my fierceness nor my naïve assumption about keeping him safe kept me from worrying, all the time.

"Our children are dying," a lay leader from a large Black Baptist church was saying. "Let this be the time that we say 'enough is enough.'" After the hour-long clench in my stomach and my jaw, her words undid me. I pulled away from the crowd to wipe tears on my sleeve, and then to pull my mask off one ear to wipe my nose.

Nathan was, at that moment, protesting with some friends in a different city. He'd Sharpied our phone numbers on his arm before leaving his house with a cardboard sign that read *Goin' to the mountaintop and not coming back.*

If I'd made a sign, it might have said *Our children are dying.*

My legs were Jell-O from the five-mile walk. The combination of the energy in the crowd and my own worry twisted my guts into knots. A friend

---

1. By Julius Lester, illustrated by Jerry Pinkney. Dial Books, 1996

offered me a ride home. This was a breach of social distancing best practice, which I tried to mitigate by sitting in the back seat with the window wide open, cold damp air on my face. We were certainly not six feet apart; I leaned hard into the car's rear passenger-side door, as far away from her as could get, a ragged Kleenex in hand.

"Don't mind me," I said. "It's just my white fragility." To me, at that moment, the phrase meant that my own emotions overwhelmed my ability to respond in any constructive way to the needs of people of color around me, needs which I would very much want to address if I weren't such a tearful, wrung-out mess.

Our children are dying. In the past, those words had always sounded like they were about other people's children, maybe far away in another country. But that day I was thinking about Nathan. My pride in him finding his place and his voice in the season of protest was overlaid with my visions of teargas, police clubs, and trucks driven angrily into crowds.

Portland is often referred to as "the whitest city in America." African Americans make up only six percent of the population of Portland, and de facto segregation makes most neighborhoods even whiter. The first settlers in Oregon Territory advocated a "whites-only" region. In 1859, Oregon became the only state to enter the Union with a Black exclusion law, introducing a new law the same year prohibiting Black people from owning property and making contracts. Portland's history of racism (a phrase most often accompanied by the adjective "painful," affixed by the liberal-progressive majority for which Portland has been known for the past several decades) includes over a dozen neighborhood covenants, written as Portland boomed between the two world wars. For example, the Laurelhurst neighborhood, a mile from our house, was developed under this 1926 covenant:

> . . . nor shall the same [developed neighborhood] or any part
> thereof be in any manner used or occupied by Chinese, Japanese
> or negroes, except that persons of said races may be employed as
> servants by residents . . .

When Nathan was still stroller age, he and I went almost every day to Laurelhurst Park, the heart of the Laurelhurst neighborhood. He fed the ducks, slid down the kiddie slide, and clamored insatiably for more and higher pushes on a worn bucket swing. I did not know about redlining back then and had heard only vague references to the postwar Vanport settlement that provided housing for Black factory workers until it flooded in 1948. I never knew how Portland's racist history bled into every corner of our city, never knew that our social-justice-oriented heavily Democratic neighborhood was built less than a century ago by people who did not welcome Blacks and would not have welcomed my family.

And if I had known that? Would I have done anything differently? Mark and I often wondered: should we have done what some—but by no means all—other adoptive parents did, and move to a Black neighborhood, join a Black church, and send Nathan to a Black preschool?

"We need to be ourselves," Mark said more than once. "This is our neighborhood. This is where his friends are." I was relieved to hear him say this. I wanted him to be right.

Like every mother of a Black child, although without the hard-won intuition born of the experience of Black mothers, I knew that it was more important for Nathan than for his white friends to be polite and careful out in public. He learned to keep his hands visible at all times, and to call people "sir" and "ma'am" if he didn't know their full names. When I was with him, people treated him well; I would learn only later that without me he was often treated with suspicion or disdain by others.

In middle school, he joined a Black student group and had a place, for the first time, to talk about his racial identity with other people of color. (When he came back from the first meeting, his only comment was: "They told us we didn't have to talk to our parents about what happened at the meeting.") In high school—a private, high-brow Episcopal school where he was the only Black student in his grade—he was tapped for the school's diversity committee and sent to several conferences.

When it came time to look at colleges, Nathan was all over the map, literally. Mark and I wanted him to be in an urban setting where he would be exposed to a wider swath of culture than white Portland had to offer. And he wanted to go to a place that had a real campus ("urban, but not too urban," he would say). Many of the students from his high school ended up at small private colleges that mirrored the degree of care and comfort of their high school. Nathan wanted something bigger than this, but not too big. He ended up at a medium-sized university in Los Angeles where he was finally in a truly multiracial setting.

He attended his university's Black Student Union meetings once or twice when he first arrived. Early on, he sat in a circle with twenty other students talking about their experiences growing up Black. He described being followed by a security guard as he wandered through a department store. The student next to him talked about his brother being shot in a gang dispute while police looked the other way. The comparison between his experience and the other student's was uncomfortable for him.

"Do you ever go back to the BSU meetings?" I asked when he was home on vacation a few years later.

"I went once, right after Trump was elected." He spoke in that clipped way he had when he really didn't want to have the conversation.

"So, how was it?"

"They go about things all wrong. They segregate themselves. That doesn't do anybody any good." This was the most he'd talked with me about these things in a long time.

"They're an affinity group with no direct action other than yelling at white people."

Throughout middle school, high school and college, Nathan's life was about learning who he was as a Black man. Having grown up in a white family and attending white schools in the whitest city in America, this was not easy. I learned later, reading his writing, that his longing to fit in was often in conflict with his growing sense of who he was as a Black man.

Beyond these writings, which he published on social media, this was a part of his life he couldn't or wouldn't share with me. I understood this completely, and at the same time, like so many mothers letting their children grow up, I felt the empty space between us. It was undoubtedly exacerbated by my white perspective when it came to Blackness.

Most of his college friends were white. Raised in white privilege but rarely benefitting from it, Nathan found that in college he was both popular and always aware of the differences between him and his friends. I knew this because he would mention it in passing ("I don't know; I just feel like I don't fit the way that they all fit with each other").

He wrote bits and pieces about his experience:

> Going to Los Angeles for college was the most eye-opening experience of my entire life. I was around people who looked like me, who looked different from me, who looked different from each other. Culture and history was exciting but then I realized that I was scared. In the melting pot that makes up LA, I didn't want anyone to know that I didn't know how to be Black. I denied my Blackness by saying "I'm me."

I visited him in Los Angeles in the fall of his senior year. His school was near the ocean; the weather was always sunny, never hot, ocean breezes making palm trees sway as if we were on a tropical island. The vegetation alone made the visits a delicious break from Portland's seasonal rain. But even better was walking across campus with my son and watching him greet dozens of people with a casual wave of his big hand and a flash of his bright politician's smile. It seemed like he knew everyone. Big man on campus.

In his university of 6,500, six percent were Black, not a huge number but a far greater percentage than the Portland schools he attended. Having gone to a small, nurturing high school, college was an adjustment. He was lonely his first semester; joining a fraternity in spite of Greek Life's reputation for overwhelming whiteness turned out to be a social lifeline for him. There was only one other Black member in the fraternity. Nathan told me this story several years later as though it had just happened.

"My first week after induction, he pulled me aside and said: 'I just want to say that you're going to want to ask me things, and you should go ahead and ask.'

"He told me to speak up if anyone ever said anything that was off, you know, that they shouldn't say. And I did. They learned that certain jokes were off limits."

I could only wonder about the jokes. What I did know was that by the time Nathan graduated, there were a handful more Black fraternity brothers. Nathan had the same conversations with them that his lone predecessor had had with him.

"I'm—you know—kind of their mentor."

As the nationwide protests continued in the weeks after George Floyd's death, I needed to find my place in the movement growing around me. I didn't want that place to be as an emotionally frail, easily triggered white mom. I had long been preaching sermons about the church's role in fighting systemic racism and dismantling white supremacy. I needed to get back to that work of preaching and teaching other white people about responsibility for our racist culture. But all I wanted to do was hold my 200-plus pound son and keep him safe.

I made a list of what I would and wouldn't do:

- I would show up whenever Black pastors put out a call to clergy to show up.
- I would teach a class on racism at my church.

- I would offer a book group, on-line, to a group of white people from the neighborhood who wanted a safe place to talk about racism and figure out their own responsibility.

- I would preach about the connections between modern-day racism and Jesus' teachings on community.

- I would not try to attend every protest.

- I would not post photos of myself at protests on social media.

- I would not check in with my son five times a day to see how he was doing.

It was important for me to realize that I could not do everything. But I *could* do *something*. There were days when I failed miserably at not calling or texting Nathan to check up on him, and other days when I needed to consult the list to remind myself that I was doing enough. But otherwise, I managed.

The first meeting of the neighborhood book group I started began with the usual combination of technological challenges and small talk. It was quite the mix of people: An eighty-year-old retired nurse who was a member of my parish, a thirty-something sociology professor from a local university, a young mom who ran a children's clothing resale shop in the neighborhood, a couple friends, half a dozen women in their seventies from my parish, and some parents from the local elementary school.

For the first twenty years of my son's life, I'd thought being his mom gave me a get-out-of-white-supremacy-free card. Then, I learned how much our family had benefited from the institution of slavery—my ancestors had made millions running textile mills in New England, child labor turning cheap slave-grown cotton into fabric. I spent a year devouring books on racism, reparations, white privilege, and everyday life for people of color in America.

I learned the difference between being a non-racist and an anti-racist.[2] Most of my family and friends in the liberal-progressive bubble that was Portland and the parts of New York and New England where we had lived described ourselves as *non-racist*. We knew that racism was for bigots and anyone who didn't vote the way we did. Many of us talked about being "color-blind," not seeing color. Being anti-racist, I learned, was something

---

2. With gratitude to Ibram X. Kendi for his teaching in *How to be an Anti-Racist* (One World, 2019) and elsewhere.

else entirely. Being anti-racist meant working to dismantle racist structures as old as America. I began talking and preaching about dismantling white supremacy. I knew the phrase made people uncomfortable, especially white Episcopalians whose denomination on both sides of the Atlantic was representative of slaveholder religion.

In the book group, I found people all along the continuum between non-racist and anti-racist.

My best friend in junior high was Black. We didn't see color, said the retired nurse in her eighties.

I'm remembering conversations I had with a Black coworker a long time ago. I cringe at how clueless I was! said a school teacher.

I'm here because I want to be a better ally, said a small business owner in the church's neighborhood.

Earlier that week in one of a dozen Zoom conversations on the subject of anti-racism work, a speaker was asked the difference between being an *ally* and being *in solidarity*. I sat up a little straighter waiting for the answer, as I'd heard so many different things recently about what some people were calling "allyship."

An ally says: "I'm going to help you with your problem," while someone looking for solidarity is with you in the problem. Solidarity says to people of color: "Racism is my problem as much as it is yours."

Back in Los Angeles, Nathan had attended a few protests but was mostly channeling his energy and new-found voice into many, many social media posts each day. One day's posts included this quote:

> *Black people don't care if u stop saying 'master bedroom' or if you remove problematic shows from decades ago from hulu. Black people want an end to police brutality and institutionalized racism. Everything else is useless pandering.*

And this one:

> *Arrest the cops who killed Breonna Taylor.*

And this one:

> *There are deep links between climate change and racism.*

His friends—nearly all white—turned to him for wisdom and guidance. Most of the time, he rose to the occasion, but he shared with me that there were moments when this was tiring. I tried not to turn him into my personal expert on all matters concerning race, but the truth was that his was the only opinion I cared about. I texted him asking him what he thought about the distinction I'd heard between "ally" and "solidarity." He replied: *Whatever. I'm not really focused on the semantics of it. Really I care more about who shows up.*

A handful of us from church decided to show up by painting "Black Lives Matter" signs and standing on the sidewalk of the busy street in front of the church.

Cars honked as they drove by, and while I initially took the honking as a sign of support for our tiny protest, I realized that they understood our signs to be a support for *them*. Most of the people who honked were people of color. Often drivers or passengers raised their fists at us in a show of solidarity. A young Black man in a sports car gave me a huge smile. A city bus driver honked her horn loudly and raised her fist. ("When the bus driver does that, they're speaking for the whole bus!" said an astute twelve-year-old who'd spray-painted his sign gold.) A Black woman with long shining braids slowed to a crawl to reach over and roll down her manual crank passenger window to yell "Thank you!"

Over the course of an hour, thousands of cars honked at us. At first it was unnerving to stand still on a sidewalk I'd traversed hundreds of times, usually moving quickly. 82nd Avenue was not a pleasant street to walk along, let alone stand on. But this was different. We were standing in solidarity. We were holding space for everyone who drove by.

What started as a one-time family-friendly sign-painting event on our front lawn in mid-June turned into a weekly Wednesday afternoon demonstration we called "Sidewalk Solidarity."

Over the weeks that we stood there, twelve to fifteen of us most Wednesdays, I realized that this sidewalk solidarity was a form of hospitality. We invited neighborhood families with young children to stand with us. We shared sign-making materials with people who came without signs. And we invited passing drivers to share solidarity with us and our message.

For every couple of hundred car horns and raised fight-the-power fits we saw one or two drivers shake their heads or even show us a middle finger. The first time this happened, a familiar feeling clenched my gut. It was not fear this time, but anger, anger that quickly sent me down the sidewalk to check on the other sign-wavers.

"Did you see that?" I asked a mom and her eleven-year-old daughter, both holding signs. Mom's sign said *Black Lives Matter*; her daughter's sign said *Love is the answer.* "You okay?"

"Oh, sure," answered the mom. "There's one in every crowd."

I was not so sanguine. If someone shook their head at my Black Lives Matter sign, did that mean he didn't think Black lives mattered? I was shaky with hot rage, rage that became part of my solidarity. It was how I was showing up.

The summer of weekly solidarity on the sidewalk was cut short by an onslaught of wildfire smoke that kept everyone indoors. We turned our attention to seeking help for those who had no indoors. Once the smoke cleared, the 2020 presidential election was in sight and 82nd Avenue became a popular thoroughfare for right-wing hate groups showing their support for Trump's agenda and the police. Reports of violence kept us off the sidewalk. *I'm not advancing the Black Lives Matter movement by getting run over by a pickup truck out there,* a colleague said.

Over the course of the year, the way I showed up changed but it was always a recipe of rage and fear: rage at our country, at a history and an ethos that produced so many trigger-happy police officers, fear for Nathan and for every mother's Black son. I didn't want to be one of those white people who stopped going to protests when the weather got bad. I continued to preach about dismantling white supremacy and I forced myself to read past the headlines into the stories I'd rather ignore, about police brutality and government complacency around the country. In our own city, protests continued, with increasing infighting among protesting groups, while little progress was made on police reform.

In the same hour that a jury in Minneapolis deliberated over the verdict for Derek Chauvin, the officer who knelt on George Floyd's neck for nine minutes, police in Columbus, Ohio, shot 16-year-old Ma'Khia Bryant seconds after arriving on the scene, with no apparent attempts at de-escalation. Multiple police shootings happened in succeeding days, as if to support the claims that the Chauvin verdict represented neither justice nor safety for Black lives.

With each story the rage burned in me and fear chilled me. There was something else as well: I could feel myself turning inward toward the half-block where my church sat, looking there for hope.

Chapter 9

Mutual Aid for Beginners

I n 2020, mutual aid was all around me in Portland and in my church building. I'd never really heard a satisfying definition, so I asked my friend Aaron to help me understand mutual aid in the context of community and the church.

I had heard Aaron talk about mutual aid in connection with work he did with rural poor and incarcerated people on the Olympic Peninsula, and in connection with the national Poor People's Campaign.

"What would you say is the scriptural basis for mutual aid?" I asked him.

"It's as old as the Book of Acts, if not older," he said.

I trusted Aaron more than almost anyone. He had a sharp eye for injustice and systemic economic inequality and was extremely articulate but was so kind and loving that I wasn't as intimidated by him as I might otherwise be. A layperson who had earned a theological degree but had, for the most part, rejected the institutional church, Aaron's life's work was offering good news to the poor in the form of employment, housing, and conversation. Although I was twenty years older than Aaron, I often said he was one of the people I wanted to grow up to be.

"The earliest Christians survived only because of mutual aid," he was saying. "If you read the stories, it was all about letting go and always thinking about the needs of those who had less."

Although it seemed I had only recently begun to hear the phrase "mutual aid" everywhere, I sensed that the concept itself was as old as human community. I googled the phrase and learned that it came into use with a 1902 essay collection by a Russian philosopher named Peter Kropotkin titled: *Mutual Aid: A Factor in Evolution.* Kropotkin's theory was that mutually beneficial cooperation and reciprocity among animals and among humans was more of a driving force for evolution than natural selection or competition. Reading about Kropotkin for the first time made me miss my father, who would of course have known Kropotkin's work and been able to describe all of its flaws and nuances.

Mutual aid first caught my attention during the Occupy Portland movement in the fall of 2011. The protest against economic inequality that began with Occupy Wall Street evolved into a tent city covering two city blocks of park that lay between the federal courthouse, the county courthouse and jail, and Portland City Hall. The urban houseless encampment that mushroomed there became a community of support, consisting of not just tents but aid stations of volunteers offering free food, clothing, medical supplies, pet care, bedding, spiritual guidance, and much more. Offerings were driven by human need.

During the Black Lives Matter protests, similar aid stations were set up in those same parks, providing barbecued ribs, first aid, referrals, masks, materials for protest signs, ear plugs, eyewash, and lots of water, always water. Mutual aid organizations' generous support for protesters was itself a protest against a system of scarcity.

When Portland—including all of the Black Lives Matter demonstrations—shut down in the late summer of 2020 because of debilitating wildfire smoke that blanketed the city and made it dangerous to go outside, all of those same mutual aid organizations quickly pivoted to provide aid for people most affected by the smoke. Volunteer medics who had been at protests every night for months shifted their focus to making sure people living outside had enough masks suitable for air filtration and gallons of drinking water. Faith leaders who had been rallying parishioners for Black Lives Matter protests instead collected masks, diapers, and baby food for undocumented berry pickers west of the city who sheltered from the smoke in trailers and barns but were afraid to visit nearby emergency shelters because of their immigration status.

One Saturday in September after the smoke cleared, I arrived at a protest in a park in North Portland. I'd checked the weather, twice, and dressed for the dry cloudy day shown on my phone, in hoodie and jeans. Within minutes of arriving, I was drenched by a sudden downpour and hung out at the edge of the crowd looking for something in my pocket to clean my glasses, which were not only fogged from my mask but also covered in raindrops.

"Hello!" sounded a friendly-but-unfamiliar voice just outside my peripheral vision. I turned to see a round smiling face behind thick glasses shadowed by a Yankees cap.

"You look like you could use a poncho," he said, offering me a sealed package with one of those clear plastic ponchos that seems to be made out of the same clear plastic as produce bags at the grocery store.

"Wow, thank you so much." The guy made my day, and the encounter was just one example of mutual aid: specific solutions to specific problems experienced by people in need, whether it was someone living in a tent in need of a flashlight, or a protester in the pouring rain in need of a poncho.

This simple encounter led me to realize that mutual aid was an aspect of radical hospitality that sidestepped all of the organizational structure I was used to from decades of church. I was steeped in what I had just recently heard called the nonprofit industrial complex: churches and nonprofit social service agencies, be they ever so humble, nonetheless were often structured to set limits on generosity and to be driven, if not by profits then by sustainability and budgets created to pay staff meager wages and offer circumscribed services, staying in whatever mission lane had been carefully developed by a board. Mutual aid was structured around generosity. Where most nonprofits and churches had organizational charts and lines defining goals and objectives, aid groups blurred edges like watercolors.

The Book of Acts contains a collection of stories thought to be compiled by Luke (who wrote the version of the Magnificat handed down through the earliest years of the Christianity), stories about the earliest leaders of the Christian church after the death of Jesus. They encounter all the challenges of any fired-up group striving to carry on the work of a beloved teacher, and they bump up against internal and external conflict and resistance. Through it all, they continue to sew the thread of Jesus' teachings of community care and the centrality of the poor.

Throughout the history of organized Christianity, people searching for a pure experience of church have looked to Acts as a model of Christian community. One passage, though, both describes the more just society many people might hope to create and serves as a stumbling block for any one in our time longing for that type of society:

> Now the whole group of those who believed were of one heart and
> soul, and no one claimed private ownership of any possessions,
> but everything they owned was held in common. There was not a
> needy person among them, for as many as owned lands or houses
> sold them and brought the proceeds of what was sold. (Acts 4:32,
> 34)

I still love reading these verses and I, like so many other comfortable
white Christians who read them, know full well that I am not going to sell
all my property or ask my husband to leave our house, liquidate our hard-
earned retirement, and live in a community that holds all things in common. But I wanted that community life—especially in a pandemic—and I
wanted to help the poor. I had to settle for the 2020 version of mutual aid
rather than the biblical version.

In the spring of 2020, I was approached in an email by a guy named
Lee who was working with a small group of restaurant workers—line cooks,
mostly—who were laid off or whose hours had been significantly cut back
because of the pandemic-related restaurant shutdown. They had come together, initially in the cramped kitchen of a small local restaurant, to make
and distribute free food from donated ingredients.

"We can't work there anymore; we need a kitchen that provides more
space," Lee said when we first talked, brushing a long straw-colored bang
off his forehead. "We need a place where we can practice social distancing.
Like in your church."

"Our kitchen fits the bill?" Like a lot of churches, our kitchen was av-
erage sized and not particularly well organized.

"Oh, yes, your kitchen is amazing!"

Wow, I thought to myself as Lee said this.

Amazing was most definitely not the first thing that came to mind
when I thought of the kitchen at Saints Peter & Paul. The cupboard doors
had been bought second-hand and hung by a well-meaning church volunteer ten years ago. The doors never quite closed correctly. Things were
in odd places: baking pans across the room from the oven, day-to-day
utensils like spatulas in the same drawer with a half-dozen nearly empty
rolls of masking tape, binder clips and bits of string that fill most people's
junk drawers at home. The cracked laminate counters had not been declut-
tered enough to clean in a very long time. An industrial-sized range hood
hummed constantly; it was the only way to keep the antique gas stove from
emitting a scary smell.

A large stainless-steel cooking island gleamed by comparison to the rest of the space, but its placement in the center of the kitchen created a bottleneck: if one person was chopping potatoes there, someone else could not stand at the sink without bumping butts.

"And what do you do, exactly?"

"People order food from our website and we prepare it. Then they pick it up or we deliver it."

It sounded too good to be true. Later I googled Lee's organization, Crisis Kitchen. Their website's home page showed a picture of five or six masked 20-somethings lined up six feet apart along the fence outside the local restaurant with the too-small kitchen. Across the top was a banner that read: *We make food and give it to hungry people.* From there I clicked through to photos of the day's offerings: tamales garnished with micro-greens, lentil soup and buttery crostini, shepherd's pie, and brownies.

From the look of it, one of their volunteers must have been an aspiring professional food photographer. Here was the kind of food porn I'd expect to find in a coffee table style cookbook or a food blog for wealthy moms with time on their hands. Instead, these delicious photos, like the food they represented, had been crafted as gifts for hungry people who were unlikely to afford the ingredients, let alone a prepared meal of such quality. Crisis Kitchen was a far cry from soup kitchens where I'd volunteered from time to time over the years, serving up minestrone and crackers. Who knew that food prepared for unhoused people could look so beautiful and taste so good? Not me, certainly, until I learned about Crisis Kitchen.

Within a few weeks they were all moved in. The church had no formal agreement with them, and I realized later that part of the mutual aid ethos was that they were not a legally recognized entity of any kind, nor did they want to be treated like one. They were energetic young people with kind and generous hearts, and I was happy to have them in the building, espe-cially during the pandemic when no one was around. We agreed that they could be in the kitchen any time that others didn't need it.

They asked about downstairs storage for dry goods and a freezer. *Why not*, I thought. The church basement was a small rabbit warren of dark rooms, each with a small window near the low ceiling, made darker by vines and weeds growing in the window wells. Like many church basements built in the 1950s, these rooms had been designed for the large Sunday school I was always hearing about from the church's oldest members. Stacks of child-sized chairs still hid in some of the corners as evidence; otherwise it was hard to imagine children in those cramped spaces. Other than a large closet packed with Rahab's Sisters supplies and one room dedicated to a small twelve-step group, the basement had been empty for years.

I periodically got an email or a text from one of the cooks asking if they could bring another refrigerator or freezer into the basement. I always replied: *Sure. Why not?* I lost track, eventually, of the number of volunteers using the space to make food for hungry people, and of the number of large appliances. One day I went down to the basement to find every inch of wall space occupied with a refrigerator, freezer, or utility shelf piled high with spices, grains, dried beans, and canned goods. The basement was organized like the dry storage area of a good-sized restaurant.

"All of the fridges have names," Adrian, one of the cooks, told me one day. "The big one in the kitchen is named Angela, for Angela Davis."

Angela had recently been a source of tension as food for Brigid's Table had been rearranged and some of it thrown out. Such was life in a church kitchen, but it seemed to be falling to me to resolve these things. This was a role I resisted mightily.

"Then there's Rosa, the big fridge downstairs where we keep milk, butter, and eggs. Rosa is named after Rosa Parks. Sojourner sits next to Rosa and is a freezer where there's stuff like frozen bagels. We keep produce in Frida, named after Frida Kahlo. She was a painter . . . "

I interrupted at one point to say "I do know who all these people are," aware as I did that I was feeling my age. I resisted saying, *I knew who those people were before you were born!*

I had my father to thank for some of my familiarity with all of these historic rabble-rousers. It was he who regularly wore a bright red t-shirt with a sketch of Emma Goldman, the anarchist activist who died in 1940, inscribed with her oft-quoted words: *If I can't dance, I don't want to be part of your revolution.* Emma was honored by Crisis Kitchen in a freezer named Big Emma.

Sometime in the summer Sharon, one of my favorite faithful church ladies, called me.

"I was talking with Linda the other day." I knew right away how this was going to go. Linda was too sweet and gentle to complain about anything to her priest. But she and Sharon had been friends for a very long time. Sharon's down-to-earth and forthright nature made her the obvious conduit between Linda's unhappiness and my ear.

"She's worried that when things open up again there won't be room for us."

"What do you think?" I asked, stalling a bit. I heard Sharon catch in her breath before answering.

"I see her point, I guess. I also know that you want to have a lot of people doing stuff in the church."

"When we worry that there might not be room for us, who do you mean by *us*?" I asked. "What if we stopped saying *them* and *us* about people who are using our space to do important good work, helping people?"

It seemed so obvious to me, but I knew I was up against the density of memories of the church in the seventies and eighties.

Sharon and I agreed that I'd share my perspective about everyone being *us* with the whole board at our next meeting. Linda was on the board and after that meeting I heard no more complaints, at least not from her. I never knew if it was because she appreciated what I said or because she realized her objections were futile. I didn't like to be in disagreement with parishioners like Linda, but I knew that the future of the church—the church's chance to be a meaningful entity in the community—depended on the kinds of relationships that I was trying to form with Crisis Kitchen and others.

Around this time Adrian, the Crisis Kitchen volunteer who spent the most time in the church building, sent me a text about a cluttered supply closet near the kitchen:

I'm thinking it would be great to have a bunch of shared supplies all in one place: like, Rahab's Sisters, Crisis Kitchen and Brigid's all use lots of to go containers. Okay if I clean up the closet where all of that is?

Sounds great, I replied. *Go for it.*

It made sense to me, and the idea of a shared source of containers fit right in with my idea of getting rid of *us* and *them*.

Little did I know that he would take a bunch of supplies for preparing Tuesday night sandwiches and put them somewhere else entirely. I knew nothing about this until Mary, one of the Brigid's Table volunteers, sent an email—what might be called a "howler" in Harry Potter's world—to Adrian about how unacceptable it was for them to reorganize the closet and move any of our stuff. It was going to take more effort than I wanted to spend on helping the church members to adjust their collective attitude.

Within a few months, in addition to the catalog of freezers and refrigerators named after 20th-century activists, Crisis Kitchen began to partner with other groups. They occasionally prepared food for Rahab's Sisters, for example, and regularly took and distributed any food Rahab's Sisters couldn't give away during deliveries to encampments of houseless people.

One Sunday afternoon, I was at the church waiting to meet a handyman for a bid on one of the eight thousand little repairs the building needed. I was happy to see three people working and chatting in the kitchen. I was often rushed when going in and out of the church while the Crisis Kitchen volunteers were working and we rarely had time to chat.

"Mmm, that looks so good!" I said, by way of greeting. "What's for lunch?"

"These are tamales. We make about three hundred of them every week," answered a tall woman as she wiped hands on a floured denim apron. "About half chicken, have vegan."

"So awesome!" I probably used that word too much, especially given that no one around me had used it for years. "I'm Sara, by the way."

I might have met them before—they looked familiar, but that might just have been their aprons and the way they leaned into their shared work around the stainless-steel island. They introduced themselves: Peter, Hannah, Sasha. I thought I would probably forget their names as soon as I heard them, so I tried the trick I'd discovered that sometimes helped:

"Tell me about your names. Did someone give it to you? Or did you choose it?" So many of the people I met in the church parking lot on Tuesdays or Fridays had made up their name halfway through their life.

"I'm named after my grandfather," volunteered Peter. "Lots of Peters in my family, not sure why," he added with a shrug.

"Sasha is my middle name. I think my mom just liked the name, thought it was pretty. My first name is Margaret, after my father's mother, but I like Sasha better." I didn't tell her that I actually thought Margaret was a lovely name; I thought it would make me seem old. (Which, compared to the three of them in their twenties and thirties, I was indeed.)

"I think I'm named after Hannah in the bible," said Hannah. "Which is weird since our family never went to church."

The conversation shifted to Crisis Kitchen and mutual aid. "I work here at the church,"

I said that a lot lately, rather than saying I was the priest or the pastor; I never knew what negative associations with clergy someone might bring to that kitchen. There were certainly plenty to choose from.

"We just love that you're all here," I continued. "It's great having the kitchen get so much use. I love knowing that so many people are being fed."

"Just so you know—" said Hannah, sliding a watermelon-sized mound of chopped onion from a cutting board into a bowl "—we're not actually with Crisis Kitchen. We're from The People's Store. We just cook in here on Sunday afternoons. We are so grateful that Crisis Kitchen lets us use their space."

Their space?

This rankled me a bit. So much for there being no *us* and *them*, I thought later. As I imagined explaining to Sharon or Linda that we had yet another group using the kitchen, I decided I wouldn't tell them about the details of the conversation.

Later that afternoon at home I learned a bit more about The People's Store. The group's mission, as posted on their website, was to *create social change through mutual aid organizing for unhoused folks.* They drove a big yellow truck around town visiting encampments of houseless people. Along with freshly made tamales, they gave out hygiene supplies and bedding. I sent them some money and a few months later was rewarded with a sheet of stickers made from colorful pen-and-ink drawings of their yellow truck, a dry tent in the rain, tamales, and the slogan: Solidarity Over Charity.

Crisis Kitchen and The People's Store were among dozens of aid organizations that sprang up in 2020 to respond first to pandemic-driven hunger and poverty, then to systemic racism and the Black Lives Matter protests, and then to displacement due to toxic wildfire smoke. Portland Free Fridge, Mutual Aid Alliance, Free Hot Soup, Free Lunch Collective, Black Unity Pdx, Portland EWOKS (for Equitable Workers Offering Kommunity Support) were just a few of the organizations that showed up to help people in need in new and contextually responsive ways. Each one of these groups was driven by a desire to break away from traditional hierarchical scarcity-based structure in order to provide hope and goodness.

Mutual aid was the place where solidarity met generosity. Or, as the director of Rahab's Sisters put it once: *If I can give it to you, I will. If I can't . . . well, that sucks.* Mutual aid meant that people and their basic needs extended beyond any boundaries of ownership or privilege.

All could be summed up by Crisis Kitchen's identity statement: *We make food and give it to hungry people.*

Solidarity, not charity. It seemed as though after I first saw that slogan on The People's Store materials, I started seeing it everywhere: bumper stickers, hashtags, and fliers on the utility poles in my neighborhood. I had been operating on a charity model for a long time, using my checkbook and Goodwill drop-offs as a way to share resources, rather than meeting people with very real needs and learning from them about those needs.

I thought about the woman I'd met at a phone booth years ago when Rahab's Sisters first started, the one who told Carol and me about flavored condoms being so much better than the cheaper tasteless ones. In that brief conversation she was not asking for charity but sharing a bit of her life with us.

Giving money was not a bad thing, but it was not giving me the connection I so longed for. Over the course of 2020 as I learned about mutual aid and got to know people through Rahab's Sisters and Brigid's Table that I would not have otherwise gotten to know, that began to change.

I knew it was changing not because I had learned the names and stories of many of the people from the streets who hung around the church. I knew it was changing because I became obsessed with sleeping bags. I knew from bringing food and supplies to people living in tents along the freeway east of the church that it was colder there than other places and that sleeping bags were in short supply. They were stolen, or easily ruined in tents flooded with heavy rain. In the fall when the rains came, I asked neighbors and friends to leave their extra sleeping bags on my porch. A few did, although not as many as I'd hoped.

"Everyone has gear they haven't gotten around to taking to Goodwill, right?" I asked a friend while we were out on a walk.

"I think that's more of a spring cleaning thing," she said. "I'll check, when I'm getting ready for summer. I'll see what I've got."

Couldn't you check now? I thought. I felt some urgency, but didn't want to guilt-trip my friends. I left it there.

I ordered some cheap sleeping bags from Amazon and brought them to church along with a handful of bags neighbors had left for me. I discovered that I loved giving away new sleeping bags. The extravagance of it reminded me of experiences I'd had at Rahab's Sisters, of serving up unexpectedly delicious food and then offering seconds.

"Wow, for me?" asked a woman named Annie, her eyes opening wide. She was living in a car she'd bought with the federal stimulus mailed to most Americans at the start of the pandemic. "I've just been sleeping under a pile of coats but it's getting cold."

In early February 2020 the local news began predicting severe winter weather. In the week before Valentine's Day the temperature dropped into the mid-thirties, the wind picked up, and the sky became thick as lead. That Monday I posted a link on Facebook for an inexpensive synthetic sleeping bag from Amazon and asked people to consider sending one or two my way.

As I ordered three bags myself, I was thinking of how windy it was even on cloudless Sunday afternoons when we brought meals to people camping along the freeway bike path. I was thinking of Tommy, whose tent was nestled against a dense hedge along the backside of the last house on the street that dead-ended at the freeway embankment. Tommy was in his mid-fifties and bore the marks of a long-term meth habit: lesions on his face and hands and an erratic twitch. He often had a young woman, Barb, sharing his tent. We never saw her, but he asked for two of everything and talked about how cold she got at night. I hadn't even met her, and I wanted her to have a sleeping bag in place of the county-issue blankets we often distributed.

My friends who had ordered sleeping bags didn't have a Tommy or Barb to think of when they ordered them, and I wondered if that made it harder for them to click on the link than it was for me.

But by Wednesday a pyramid of sleeping bags sat in my living room and the recycle bin outside overflowed with the Amazon boxes they came in.

Wednesday night I met a couple of Rahab's Sisters volunteers in the church parking lot to caravan out to check on people in encampments, people we had come to think of as ours. Over the course of the day, in addition to my pile of sleeping bags we'd collected a case of air-activated hand warmers, and several large boxes of donated hats, gloves, blankets, and winter coats. Crisis Kitchen put a huge pot of homemade soup into a thick-walled Styrofoam box, the kind made for shipping fresh fish on ice across the country. Starbucks donated several boxes of hot coffee. We made carafes of hot chocolate and loaded it all into our three cars along with stacks of containers for soup and hot drinks.

The wind was sharp along the freeway where we found our people, some in tents and some in cars. There were Mary and Gary, who camped on the wide sidewalk across the street from a large subsidized apartment building. Mary and Gary were sort of the den parents of the group; they knew where everyone else was and what they needed. They shared a large tent up on palettes which kept it dry in heavy rains, and it was layered over with tarps that kept the wind out. On Sunday afternoons Mary was often out sweeping the sidewalk in front of their tent. It was always tidy, everything in its place.

There were three of us in the caravan that night. I had the huge cooler of hot soup in the back of my Subaru, sleeping bags piled around it and boxes of donated sweaters and gloves in the back seat. Connor had the hot chocolate, coffee, and hand warmers. A guy named Dave had coats and blankets. We pulled up alongside Mary and Gary's tent. A light glowed from inside. Through the crack left by the tent's broken zipper I could see, with some relief, that the light was from a battery-operated lantern, not a propane one. (I had recently heard several horror stories about tent fires.)

We opened our hatchbacks as a handful of people crept out of their tents. It was dark and the wind was picking up.

"Want some soup?" I asked Mary.

"No, thanks, hon," she answered, reaching a hand up behind her head to adjust the comb holding her hair. "We just finished a big pot of chili. But these guys—" she waved to the tent next to her, "they aren't home but they really need batteries and blankets."

"No batteries, I'm afraid." Batteries were a small thing but I hated not having something that someone needed. But I was learning that was part of the solidarity of mutual aid. I remembered Anneliese's words: *If I can give it to you, I will. If I can't, that sucks.* The pang of disappointment I felt about not having any batteries was me being in solidarity, sharing a "that sucks" moment with Mary and her absent neighbors.

"We do have lots of blankets, though. Can we leave them here with you?"

"Of course, hon, I'll make sure they get them." I loved it that Mary, the curbside den mother, called everyone *hon*, and I was part of everyone.

While I was helping Mary pick out blankets for her neighbors, a group of people had gathered around the car with the soup, which Connor ladled into pint to-go containers with impressive speed.

"You definitely want to keep the lid on so it stays hot," he said to a young guy missing his front teeth.

"You kidding? I'm going to eat it right now. But can I get another to take to the guy next to me?"

"Of course, my man," Connor replied. "Need anything else?"

After a few minutes, the small crowd dissipated, most people laden with armloads of blankets, socks, containers of hot soup, whatever we had to give that might protect them from the cold and snow.

I realized as we drove away that people like Mary were also practicing mutual aid, looking after her neighbors when by the world's standards she herself had nothing.

This same scene repeated itself at another four or five stops. When we got back to the church and unloaded the stuff we had left, I felt more anxious than when we started. We had probably interacted with thirty people in the course of two hours. Who else was out there? Who else would be cold that night?

"I wish we didn't have so much left over," I said to Connor. "I know there are people who need it." I was thinking of the people who had not been home in their tents when we'd stopped by, and people on blocks we hadn't even visited.

"I know, but it's something. We gave them something." He was pouring what was left of the soup, still steaming hot, into a smaller container that would fit into the refrigerator.

That night at home in bed I thought about how many people had hats, or blankets, or a new coat or sleeping bag, that hadn't had them when we arrived. It had to be enough, and yet as the wind buffeted our sturdy old house I couldn't stop thinking about Tommy and Barb in their tent. They were no longer simply "houseless people." They were part of the church community.

Mutual aid, I had learned, was all about solidarity. But solidarity also meant that once the weather turned bad, sleepless nights became the norm in my house.

Chapter 10

Hunger

For much of 2020, the greatest hunger I felt was for communion bread. It was, after all, the bread and wine of communion, known in churchy circles as Holy Eucharist, that had hooked me, years ago, when I first met Ed McIntyre and started attending the church where he was priest. On a Thursday afternoon midsummer thirty-five years ago I slid into one of the dark wood pews of the small side chapel at Saint Stephen's in downtown Portland. The place had that church smell of old wood, candle wax, and dust from the rough fabric that covered the kneelers. I was wearing a cotton skirt and it was so hot in the chapel that it felt as though my thighs were sticking to the wood even through the thin fabric.

I timed my arrival so I wouldn't have to talk to anyone before the service started. There were four other women in the pews, all of them older than me. One was a petite redhead with a white cane whom I'd seen feeling her way through Sunday church. I'd seen the others the previous Sunday as well, with their silver hair and black purses, light sweaters across their shoulders even in the heat.

I was shy and new—I had hated being new anywhere ever since my parents moved me to a different school for third grade and all the other kids seemed like they had never not known each other. I hadn't gotten to the point where I knelt in public the way I'd seen others do in the first few minutes before church, but I leaned forward and rested my forehead on the back of the pew in front of me, my hands on either side.

I was newly transplanted to Portland in a newish marriage destined for the trash heap. I had been baptized two years earlier and was still finding my way into faith. What pulled at me most back then were the mysterious parts, things that I didn't understand but that continued to draw me in like a miner following a vein of iron ore in the dark.

This, Father Ed was saying, holding up a large communion wafer, *is my body, which is given for you. Do this for the remembrance of me.*

Then he lifted the silver goblet of wine and said, *Drink this, all of you: This is my blood of the new Covenant. Whenever you drink it, do this for the remembrance of me.*

He had his back to us. He wasn't talking to us, he was talking to God. The words he said about the bread and wine, the body and blood—he was reciting a story and making an offering, imitating Jesus, because that's what Jesus commanded. A wave of understanding thrilled through me, a shiver in that heat.

I stood there and I got it. Jesus was there in the bread and wine and in the priest. This sharing of bread and wine, whether in a tiny chapel service on a Thursday afternoon or in a grand cathedral on a Sunday morning was part of what it meant to be church. The ritual—which I had learned was based on an actual meal and, presumably, actual words Jesus said, had endured over so many centuries, changing and unchanging—drew me in. I didn't know how the mystery of the Eucharist "worked," but I wanted to be part of it.

The altar, a slab of dark oak against the chapel wall, was at the same time a table where everyone was welcome, even me with my awkward newness. I felt actual hunger gnawing at me—it was close to dinnertime—and I felt the hunger for understanding, connection, and belonging. I had a feeling that I could get fed with all of that at that table.

The priest turned from the altar to face us, the small silver plate with the wafers in one hand and the silver chalice in the other. "The gifts of God for the people of God," he said, holding up the bread and wine, an offering of grace. Now he was talking to us.

I slid sideways out of my pew, thinking simultaneously that it felt good to move and that it was too hot to do so. My neck was damp with sweat, and I could feel beads of sweat on my forehead. At the end of my pew, before coming forward, I gave a little nod toward the altar as I'd seen others do, symbolic of a bow of reverence before approaching God's holy table. I knelt at the altar rail, which was just wide enough for the five of us who were present that afternoon to receive at once. I snuck a glance at the others, our hands cradled one in the other, lifted up to the priest. Some of the ladies bowed their heads; others looked up at Father Ed as he gave them communion.

I listened to the words, repeated five times:

> *The body of Christ; the bread of heaven.*
> *The blood of Christ; the cup of salvation.*

The rhythm of the words grounded me, as did the taste of that papery wafer, dipped in port wine and melting on my tongue. Wordsworth's words came to me: . . . *in this moment there is life and food for future years.*

Little did I know at that moment just how much life and food was in that small, mysterious ritual meal.

In an oh-so-mysterious way, there was a connection between these wafers and the church's ability to change the world. It changed me. All of a sudden, it hit me: I wanted to be the one at that altar, saying those prayers. I wanted to be the one to say: *the gifts of God for the people of God* and invite people to that table or any table, communion with the mysterious and the holy and also—especially—communion with one another. I wanted to be the one dishing out the wafers, feeding people with the Body of Christ even if I had only a vague idea of what all of that might mean. I thought it meant that there in that small dark space, we were strangers to one another and yet by receiving that grace being handed out at the rail we became a community. Perhaps we would be sent out to feed others, or simply to experience that generosity of communion in other places.

Back in my pew, I knelt on the kneeler, bare knees against that rough fabric. Shuddering through me on that sweaty Thursday afternoon was the thought that this mini-meal of bread and wine might, indeed, have power to change the world.

In the summer of 2020, mid-pandemic, I began giving communion at the church, by appointment, to one household at a time. Few people took me up on my offer—most parishioners either wanted to wait for "real church," or were staying home until they were vaccinated. But a few came.

One was Katherine, whose daughter Jeannie brought her. Katherine was eighty-nine, and had been a member of Saints Peter & Paul for sixty years. She had curly white hair, wire-rimmed glasses, and eyes that twinkled and darted around, as if compensating for her ears which had, for the most part, stopped working several years earlier. I had set up two chairs in front of the altar about twenty feet away. I lit the candles and put on a long white robe and a green stole—green was the liturgical color for that time of year which the church calendar calls "Ordinary Time" and which I call "the long, green, growing season."

I had set out prayer books and a little leaflet with instructions and responses for the stripped-down service we were about to do.

"I'm so glad you're both here," I said when they got settled in their red chairs. "If you weren't here, there would be no reason for me to be here, and I'm so happy to be here." It was one of those things I liked to say to congregations, but it sounded a little silly said to my congregation of two.

"Katherine, would you like to do a reading?" Katherine shook her head with a smile. I asked Jeannie the same question.

"Oh, no, I'm not one of those. I just like to listen."

Okay, then.

I prayed the opening prayer, read a snippet from scripture, and proceeded to what I always reminded people was the "main event," the Holy Eucharist.

The preponderance of churchgoers might think the main event is the sermon but in liturgical churches that offer the sacrament, they would be wrong. Yet another reason I hated Zoom church so much: it was half a service at best.

On the night before he died for us, our Lord Jesus Christ took bread, blessed it, broke it, and shared it with his friends, saying: take, eat; this is my body. There was no wine to be shared during pandemic times so this bread—or rather, these wafers, a poor substitute—would need to suffice as the taste of Jesus I had to offer.

As our savior Christ has taught us, we are bold to say . . . Our Father, who art in heaven, hallowed be thy name . . .

As with worshippers always and everywhere, whether in a church pew, nursing home, hospital bed, or jail cell, Katherine and her daughter perked up for the Lord's Prayer and joined in. The words are etched in most people's memories even if they haven't been to church for years or cannot remember their prayers from one week to the next.

The gifts of God for the people of God. I said, just as every priest did every time the Eucharist was celebrated.

I held up two wafers, put them on a silver saucer, and pushed it toward the other side of the altar. I stepped back about eight feet, arms outstretched, and invited them forward to help themselves. Self-service communion is not my favorite, but it was what was called for. As they came forward, Katherine holding onto Jeannie's arm, Jeannie pausing for a second to lean on the communion rail as they ascended the single step to the altar, I said: The body of Christ; the bread of heaven.

I was not too far away to miss the tears in Katherine's eye. Jeannie, usually tough as nails, smiled at her mother's emotion and at me. Communion will do that to you, even in a pandemic.

The last time I broke actual bread and shared it as eucharistic bread was March 1, 2020. March 8 was a regular church service but by then the bishop had dictated that we use wafers instead of bread. While it may not have actually been true, the tiny, sterile-tasting wafers gave the impression of being more sanitary than the home-baked bread my congregation was used to. By March 16, all churches were closed.

I had half a dozen occasions over the course of the pandemic to say mass and hand out communion wafers that were as sterile as my sanitized hands and medical-grade mask. I was grateful for the opportunity to connect with people that way, especially parishioners like Katherine whom I otherwise would not have met, because she did not have a computer and her hearing made telephone visits impossible. But it was a far cry from taking a loaf of bread someone had made from flour, water, salt and honey the day before (or, if one was lucky, that same morning) and breaking it in half, holding the broken pieces in the air and inhaling the bread's fragrance while maybe a tiny crumb or two fell to the linen cloth below.

The body of Christ should taste like heaven but not like dessert, someone once said. My favorite communion bread included a generous amount of honey. The honey did double duty; it made the bread sweet and made it moist. The best communion bread was chewy enough to be substantial, but not so much so that one felt like they were chomping on Jesus for hours.

I had served several churches where the bread was so delicious that as I distributed it at the altar rail part of me wanted to say: *wait until you taste this—it's so good!* instead of the usual *the Body of Christ; the bread of heaven.* Experiences of delicious homemade communion bread taught me that it was important for church to leave a delicious taste in one's mouth.

I thought communion bread should be delicious and I myself loved to eat delicious food, but the idea I learned from Crisis Kitchen, that food prepared for the very poor should always taste delicious, was new to me. I had volunteered in several soup kitchens over the years, and no one in charge ever cared about the taste. We thought we should get points for food that was both warm and nutritious, and we left it at that.

Part of my family's culture on my mother's side was our ambiguous relationship with food. Yes, food should taste delicious, and yes, it was to be enjoyed, but not too much, especially if one were female.

Having enough to eat was never an issue. My family always had enough, as did I when I was on my own. I cannot remember a single moment of being hungry in the sense of not knowing where the next meal would come from. Food insecurity or food scarcity were neither terms nor concepts that held any meaning for me until I began meeting people in churches who did not have enough to eat.

Imprinted on me long before then were my grandmother's stories about the dangers of overeating. My grandmother was known for telling stories, and for telling the same stories over and over again. She had a raspy voice from years of smoking strong unfiltered cigarettes. Summer mornings around the breakfast table often provided an opportunity for a story.

"There's some de-*licious* oatmeal on the stove," my mother offered one morning the summer I was nine.

I hated oatmeal, especially when my mother said it was good for me.

"Can I just have some milk and an English muffin?" My favorite, with butter filling up the nooks and crannies just like in the TV commercials.

"'May I?' you mean," said my mother. "Yes, you may."

The toaster-oven was plugged into an ancient light fixture in the dining room and there was an elaborate combination of things that all needed to work together in order for the toaster to work. The whole arrangement frightened me.

"Could you do it for me, pleeease?" I asked my mother.

"Sure. But don't whine like that."

"You know," my grandmother said, as I poured myself a second glass of milk, "watching you reminds me of a story I heard once."

I knew what was coming.

"There was an Ethiopian emperor who liked his wives fat as seals, wallowing around on the ground, and so he fed them milk all day long. They grew and grew, and eventually they became so fat they couldn't move. They got their milk in tubes."

The image of these women fat as seals and unable to move scared me, but I still wanted the second glass of milk.

I looked to my mother for support. I knew she didn't like the story, but she wouldn't say anything.

She turned to me and said, "One glass is all you really need."

"How come Mark gets to eat a whole box of Cap'n Crunch?" I asked about my brother.

"He's a growing boy," my mother answered. "He can eat whatever he wants."

I remember riding in a hot car on a July afternoon a year or two later, looking at the way my thighs spread out on the sticky car seat. I thought about the seal-shaped wives of that mythical African king and wondered if that's where I was headed. I felt shame flush through my face and neck. My thighs were never actually as large as my shame and self-consciousness. Like many women in my family, I got my period early, accompanied by a bosom which, as it swelled to what my mother called "grown-up sized" while I was still a child, filled me with shame as well.

"When I was your age," my grandmother said to me once when I was thirteen, "I weighed one hundred and eighty pounds." She took a drag of her cigarette. "And do you know how I took it off?"

"You walked—" I started, because I knew the story; she'd told it many times.

"I walked five miles to school every day," she cut me off. She had to tell the story. "All the way from Beacon Hill to the Winsor School in Chestnut Hill." She stubbed her cigarette out in the empty shell of the soft-boiled egg she'd finished a moment earlier.

Granny had three granddaughters and half a dozen great nieces. She told stories like this to us girls whenever the opportunity arose, which was usually whenever one of us appeared to be enjoying our food in spite of tending, as women in my family did, "to hips and thighs." The result is that most of us struggled with weight and self-image on and off for years.

"Tut, tut," my mother said to me at a family dinner while I was home from college. I had just followed my brother's lead in helping myself to seconds on dessert. "Tut, tut."

No second helpings was the rule for women in my family. Living in a college dorm and then my own small apartment, I'd obviously forgotten. Taking seconds was something one just didn't do, if one were female, unless one was making a sacrifice by taking the last bit of green vegetable so whoever was cleaning up didn't have to deal with it.

It is ironic that our family, a family that lived a lifetime, generations of lifetimes, without food insecurity and without a single moment of physical hunger, passed down to its women such a sense of personal scarcity when it came to enjoying food. This tension between abundance and scarcity may be a uniquely American experience, although it is no means an experience shared by all Americans.

In 2020, nearly fifty million Americans lived with food insecurity. Half of these people were living in poverty before the pandemic and therefore hunger was a regular experience, while others became food insecure because of pandemic-related job layoffs and other losses.

2020 became, for even the most secure, a year of scarcity. At first the burning question was: would there be enough hand sanitizer and masks to go around? Initially, it seemed the answer was no. I made masks for Mark and Nathan and in early April stood in line at the nearby Rite Aid to get there when they opened at 8am on Monday mornings, the day they got their weekly shipment. I did this not because any hand sanitizer was available, but because each shipment contained a few bottles of rubbing alcohol. I mixed it with liquid soap and lavender oil to make homemade sanitizer that burned our hands even as it promised safety.

Stores ran out of toilet paper in the first hour of every day for months. I had been a TP hoarder from way back, and our move from Seattle to Portland in mid-March included a couple large cartons of it. We had several dozen rolls on hand for most of that shortage, but I snapped up an extra package now and then during my Monday morning Rite Aid visits.

The first year of pandemic life was chronicled by shortages and scarcity. A flour shortage reflected the impulse of newly home-bound people to bake more. A shortage of home exercise equipment meant that gyms were closed and people working from home wanted to work out. A couple months into the pandemic, hair clippers were in short supply. After the murder of George Floyd and the renewed public outcry over systemic racism, books on the subject were hard to get for weeks. As more people ventured out late at night to protest police brutality, and as police responded with an increasingly liberal use of tear gas, there was a run on gas masks.

These gas masks came in handy with the wildfires of late August, 2020, when home air purifiers were needed and suddenly impossible to get. In the fall and winter, when households like mine set up outdoor patio spaces complete with propane heaters and canopies so they could invite friends over for happy hour in a safe way, propane cannisters flew off their outdoor shelves as quickly as they came in.

In Oregon, the number of people who became food insecure in 2020 grew to twenty-five percent of the overall population. The percentage of Black and Latino Oregonians affected was higher. I never knew, when I came across such statistics, whether they even included people without addresses, people living in tents or in their cars. The women we saw at Rahab's Sisters were tough and resilient, but they were getting hungrier.

They lined up early at the gate to the church's back yard where we'd set up canopies and a scattering of chairs. On the whole, their faces were drawn, and like the rest of us, those who usually wore make-up were wearing less, or none at all. The parish hall inside where they used to sit and visit around tables was a sterile assembly line of hot food containers and snack bags. Masked volunteers brought food out to the guests one shopping bag at a time.

"There's dinner for you in here," said a volunteer named Katy as she handed the bag to Sandy, one of our regulars who was housed in a large "manor" for low-income seniors nearby.

"Thank you." Sandy's mask sagged below her nostrils. Then she put a hand on Katy's wrist and added, "can I have two bags, please? I don't know when Meals on Wheels is coming back."

"Of course," said Katy.

I watched all this, glad Katy knew to say yes even though I knew we were about to run out of food. The kitchen crew had already talked about ordering pizza, and another volunteer was foraging in the Crisis Kitchen pantry for cans of soup.

"Do you have any cake?" Sandy asked Katy when she came back with a second dinner. She was in her late forties but her voice was high like a child's.

"Oh, I'm so sorry, I don't think we have cake." Both volunteer and guest looked positively crestfallen at the news; both saying and hearing no was harder during the pandemic.

The people who came to Rahab's Sisters on Friday nights, and who lined up in the church parking lot for sack suppers on Tuesdays, experienced hunger in different ways. They were hungry not just for nutrition but for the sweetness of community, the opportunity to sit down with friends. We all hungered for that.

During the epic journey to the promised land as told in the Old Testament book of Numbers, a dense cloud leads the people through the wilderness. The whole idea of being led by a cloud fascinated me; wouldn't one rather be led by something like a light or a flag? But no, during that long ordeal, the people are led by a cloud. Sometimes the cloud stops in one place for days; sometimes it moves through the night. The people never know. This uncertainty is not unlike the uncertainty of the pandemic. The shortages of necessities, the varying availability of things like masks, toilet paper, and hand sanitizer, the ever-changing nature of what people needed most—all of this was like that cloud.

One night at Rahab's Sisters I chatted with someone named Alissa who lived in a tent on a freeway embankment. I knew that her tent had been stolen a few weeks earlier and was glad to see she had a new one at her feet.

"I'm really struck by how many tents we give away," I said. "I know that they sometimes get stolen.

"Yeah, the good ones get stolen, and the cheap ones fall apart. You need to put tarps on them to keep the wind out, but too many tarps will bend the poles and they collapse."

We received donations of many twenty-five-dollar Amazon tents. Now I understood that they weren't all that great.

"The big thing is fires. Hand sanitizer fires."

"Hand sanitizer fires?" We gave out lots of hand sanitizer when we went out on deliveries. We were always so pleased that our houseless friends and neighbors were so into hand sanitizer.

"Yup. You cut it open and light it under a soda can. You cut the top off the can and fill it with water. One of those little bottles of hand sanitizer will burn for four minutes. Just enough to boil water." She paused and took a bite of the quiche I'd brought her a few minutes earlier.

My awareness of how people cooked and ate while living in tents and under tarps on the edges of parking lots and freeways was limited. Alissa proceeded to expand my horizon of understanding.

"My favorite stove is made out of a Dinty Moore beef stew can. You put the sanitizer in an open can underneath or, if you're lucky, a couple of cans strung together with wire." Her eyes, often half-shut by weed, sparkled as she spoke. "Then you fill the Dinty Moore can with water, and float, say, an empty large size tuna can on top. It's like a double boiler and a non-stick frying pan all rolled into one."

"Wow!" I said. "I'm learning so much!"

"I don't know if you know I used to be a chef," she said, her mind visibly turning from stove mechanics to memory.

"Yes, I remember." A few weeks earlier while we were out doing Sunday afternoon camp deliveries, Alissa had regaled several of us with stories of meeting Anthony Bourdain. The stories might have been imaginary, but there was as much truth in it as there was ingenuity in making a stove from a Dinty Moore can.

The stove conversation was enlightening and also an important reminder that the people we saw for dinner on Friday nights had whole lives the rest of the week, and before they found their way to living in a tent or hanging out at the church on 82nd Avenue. In another time, Alissa could perhaps have prepared the dinner we were sharing, and probably much more.

We often started our Sunday afternoon deliveries at the Methodist church around the corner from Saints Peter & Paul where half a dozen tents and the same number of cars took up much of a block. Diane was in her early sixties and lived in a large twelve-year-old SUV with her forty-something son, Stanley. One Sunday we pulled up a few car-lengths away as she came out of her car.

"Hey, Diane, want some dinner?" asked Kaylyn, the day's lead person for our caravan. That was always our greeting when we approached houseless people; it was a way of letting them know right away what we were and were not about.

"You've got a choice between chili, cornbread, and salad, or lasagna and salad. The chili has meat; the lasagna is vegetarian. The lasagna just came out of the oven and it smells amazing. And there's cherry pie for dessert."

Diane looked a little furrowed as she heard all this. She wore her hair long and blond, and had a habit of twisting a curl against her shoulder whenever she was listening or deep in thought.

Kaylyn added: "You can have both, you know."

Diane's face relaxed and broke into a smile.

"Oooh, now I feel like a queen!"

We left her and Stanley with double helpings of everything. Making Diane feel like a queen had made my day.

Later on the same Friday when I'd watched Katy hand Sandy her extra dinner, I was chatting with volunteers stocking snack bags for the following Sunday and saw one of them cutting up a sheet cake with creamy frosting.

"Oooh, yum, where is that going?" I asked. The frosting was making my mouth water.

"Everyone got cookies with their dinner tonight and we don't have a lot of dessert planned for Sunday so we thought we'd box this up" said a volunteer named Dylan as he spatula'd the cake into small to-go boxes.

"Could I snag a couple of those and a couple of forks?" It was late in the evening and most of the guests outside had left so I didn't think I'd cause too much trouble.

Sandy was still outside; she was often one of the last to leave. There was an empty chair near her under the pop-up canopy that protected us from a light drizzle. I was glad I had several layers on.

"Look what I found inside," I said, handing her a box and a fork. "This is for you."

She opened up the box with the care and wonder of a child expecting a precious gift.

"Oh, thank you!" Her eyes lit up. "Is this really for me?"

"All for you. May I?" I gestured to the chair next to hers. She patted it enthusiastically. I moved it a few inches away, although admittedly outdoors on Friday nights, we all sat closer together than the CDC advised.

I opened the second box of cake, pulled my fork out of my coat pocket, and slid it through the frosting and took the first delicious bite, and then another. I looked up at Sandy and we smiled at the same time.

"So good," she said.

"So good," I replied, feeling full for the first time in a while.

Chapter 11

Ring the Bells
That Still Can Ring

T he church bell at Saints Peter & Paul had been broken for years, and no one knew why. Over the first months of my time there I tried to figure out what was wrong. This was not easy: the bell tower was small and no more than two stories off the ground, but it sat at the peak of a steeply pitched roof, and took either someone not afraid to maneuver up the side of the roof or a taller ladder than what you find in a typical church boiler room. I paid a fearless twenty-something eco-hipster to scramble up the church's isosceles-triangle roof. He got there but couldn't get enough of a purchase to pry open the louvered door of the cupola. I found a local handyman with a ladder tall enough to get there, only to discover that the little door into the cupola had been fastened shut with metal flashing in a manner that only a roofer could figure out.

I wanted the church bell fixed because I wanted our church to participate in all the bell ringing that happened in 2020. Early on in the pandemic, bells rang every night at seven o'clock in gratitude for the essential workers, initially hospital workers, and then, as the pandemic weeks marched on, for grocery-store workers, bus drivers, janitors, and Amazon delivery people—everyone who had work to do in the world so the rest of us could stay safely home. Church bells rang and neighbors banged pots and cheered. After a while, I think we all just wanted a reason to come out onto our steps and porches to make noise together. I wanted our little neighborhood church to make its own noise, if only as a way of saying: *We're here, too. We're alive and well. We care about all of you, too.*

Later, those bells tolled for death: when pandemic deaths passed certain milestones, when Ahmad Arbery was killed while out jogging, when George Floyd was killed by a police officer who knelt on his neck for eight minutes and forty-eight seconds. We stood on the sidewalk with our signs, and I was grateful, if occasionally frightened, that our church stood on such a busy street where thousands of passing drivers could see our signs. But our church bell was silent.

Bells tolled when the death toll in the United States due to COVID-19 passed a hundred thousand. I wondered, if we had a church bell, how long we would ring it to mark that hundred thousand. A hundred thousand times? One chime for every thousand deaths? When the death toll passed half a million, I didn't hear anything about bells. I imagined that our collective national grief overwhelmed that impulse, or perhaps we were simply tired of having reasons to ring bells. In September 2020, many churches rang their bells each day at noon counting down a hundred days until the November presidential election.

Every time I learned of these various bell-ringing-in-solidarity movements, I felt a twinge of FOMO—fear of missing out—on the part of my church. I couldn't wait until our bell was fixed.

It took nearly a year, but we finally got the bell fixed, a few days before Easter 2021. I was in my office at the church, where I had a door to the outside. It was one of those sunny days in late March when the temperature soared for a few hours in the afternoon. I opened my office door onto the sunny church lawn. Handymen working on the roof had been carrying ladders back and forth outside my window throughout the afternoon, fixing some gutters and replacing some shingles that had been missing for years, covering bare patches in the roof that had church leaders wringing their hands and neighbors texting us to let us know we had a problem. All of this was important maintenance and repair that had been deferred too long, but what I really cared about was the bell.

Late in the afternoon I heard clanging that reminded me of the long-handled spoons on pots that our three- and five-year-old neighbors hand banged before going to bed in the early days of the pandemic. It took me several seconds to realize it was our bell. I went out to the front of the building to find the workers to whom I owed my thanks.

"Wow! I cannot tell you how long I've been waiting for this!" I said to the roofer and his assistant who stood in the parish hall where the bell pull hung inside a narrow cupboard.

"Happy Easter!" the guy said. Like a lot of people who worked mostly outside, his mask hung below his face around his neck, so I could see several teeth missing from his smile.

"Well, it's still Lent, actually," I said, playing the church nerd never passing up an opportunity to educate an innocent bystander about the Church calendar, "but I'll take it!"

"You gotta treat it the right way," he explained, "or you're going to have to get me back up on that ladder again, and neither one of us wants that."

He took the white rope in one hand and waved the other like a conductor.

"You need to pull it gently and keep a rhythm. Allow it to swing all the way back before pulling it again."

Who knew the church bell would be so temperamental? I pulled it a few times. *Clang-clang. Clang-clang.* It was not loud, not a large, resonant gong, but then again, it wasn't a very large bell tower. The bell was probably the size of a kettle.

I had been looking forward, for months, to an outdoor worship service for the Saturday night before Easter Sunday. We would gather the day before, for Good Friday, a small gathering for the solemn service marking Jesus' betrayal and death. The Easter Vigil on Saturday night would be something entirely different: it was a long, involved liturgy that would include Holy Eucharist and a chance to ring that church bell.

The church bell notwithstanding, the night was a final reminder of all that had changed over the past year. Not least, I had walked away from the sublime Easter Vigil liturgy of my Seattle church, my favorite service of the year, as ethereal and beautiful as my new church was scrappy and rough around the edges, especially when we gathered for big feast days.

The Easter Vigil is still my favorite service of the year. On our scruffy corner of 82nd and Pine, I might have been looking forward to ringing the church bell more than anything else. I wanted to ring it—or find someone else to ring it—at the part in the service when the priest (that would be me) says *Alleluia, Christ is Risen!* just as all the lights come on. I wondered whether I would ring the bell again at the end of the night, or whether it would be too late for the neighbors, including those who slept in pick-up trucks just on the other side of the fence from where we'd be worshipping.

Then I tried to picture myself running inside to where the bell-pull hung sequestered within its rudimentary enclosure. Perhaps I'd delegate this to someone else, although I wasn't sure who that would be. Now that it was working, the bell continued to occupy my thoughts.

My theme song for this season-of-waiting-for-the-church-bell was probably the refrain of Leonard Cohen's "Anthem," *Ring the bells that still can ring* . . . I had a young cousin who had had these words tattooed on her arm:

> Ring the bells that still can ring
> Forget your perfect offering
> There is a crack, a crack in everything
> That's how the light gets in

I loved every word of this and had wondered about it for a tattoo of my own. The words were indeed a good description not just of waiting for church bells to ring but of the season of my life that coincided with everything that happened in 2020.

Although I dismissed the "ring the bells" refrain as having too many words for my own skinny arms, in the summer of 2020 I did begin to daydream about a pandemic tattoo. I imagined a Black power fist breaking through that iconic cartoon-like spiky coronavirus that was a feature of so many news articles early in 2020. Or that same fist styled as a rose—as in Portland, the City of Roses—as a memento of the summer protests. I had that design on a hoodie I'd bought on the street in June. I already had flowers on my left calf; why not something floral on the right?

I ran my tattoo ideas past my husband and son. Mark never expressed an opinion on such things, but asked: "How many is that?"

I had seven.

My first tattoo was a Celtic knot in the blues and greens of the stained-glass windows at my Seattle church. The "Trinity Knot," or Triquetra, is made up of a circle threaded through each of three interconnected leaf shapes called *vesicae piscis*. The image depicts the Holy Trinity for anyone who wants to see it that way; for those who don't, it's a lovely collection of overlapping, encircled circles and semi-circles. A safe bet for a first tattoo. People asked me: *What is that? Is that Celtic? Are you Irish?* I kept waiting for someone to ask me to explain the Holy Trinity, but it never happened.

I had one of my favorite Bible verses tattooed on my bicep: Isaiah 58:6. I would tell people that the tattoo served two purposes. First, it would force me to keep that verse planted in my memory when people asked: *Is not this the fast that I choose: to loose the bonds of injustice, to undo the thongs of the yoke, to let the oppressed go free, and to break every yoke?* The verse reminded me that faith is not about deprivation, but about justice and hope. Second, I hoped having a tattoo on the inside of my arm would motivate me to keep my bicep strong and sculpted. Every time I showed it to someone I made a muscle, hoping that it would gather up all the loose skin. Underneath, the 60-something-year-old flesh puckered like cellulite. Try as I might, of course, I had less and less control over such things.

The verse sums all that I believe in about God. Like so much of the Old Testament, Isaiah 58 is a passage of *not this, but that.* Not ostentation, but sacrifice. Not bondage, but liberation. Not self, other. Not sorrow, joy. All of this I wanted to believe and act out at every moment; all of this was light and clarity in the midst of the normal ambiguities of life.

Bonnie Raitt wrote a love song in the 1990s that included the line "Let's tattoo Bible quotes across both our hips." Perhaps any tattoo is an act of love. For me, it was also an act of hope. I hoped the text on my arm would keep me accountable to my beliefs and point my moral compass in the right direction. I hoped it would be a bell that still could ring.

It was also when I decided I wanted the words from the Magnificat, the Song of Mary, inked in concentric ovals around an icon of the two pregnant women. I abbreviated the words to their essence: *My soul proclaims the greatness of the Lord who casts down the mighty and lifts the lowly. The hungry are filled; the rich are sent away empty.* In the icon I chose, they are holding onto each other in wonderment at being chosen, in the man's world they inhabit, to each be the bearer of such great things. My Magnificat tattoo was a commitment to my own deep hope that Mary knew whereof she spoke. As a clergywoman paid to articulate faith for those around me, it seemed like this icon-in-flesh might be an inspiration to others as well as to me.

I was learning, one tattoo at a time, about finding the right self-expression for the right moment or the right year, marking time, connecting with the world in the way that a baseball connects with an outfielder's mitt. If there was an addiction to getting tattooed, it was that itch to find the image, the phrase, the truth of a particular time and place.

I was about ten years older than Mary, the curbside den mother of many tents, whom we often found sweeping outside her tent when we delivered food and supplies on Sunday afternoons. She was camped on the wide sidewalk at the base of the freeway embankment, flanked by three or four other tents on each side. The first time I met Mary it was summertime, and she was wearing short shorts on top of her large, heavily tattooed thighs. She had a couple of misshapen hearts shot through with arrows, and some initials.

"I love all your ink!" I said while handing over a couple gallon jugs of water.

"Thanks. I do them all myself." That would explain the muted colors and thick, wavy lines. "They're for my kids."

That explained the initials. "Up there, too," she said, putting down one of the water jugs and pointing a thumb behind her.

Behind her tent was a concrete stairway to a bit of fence over the freeway. I squinted into the western sun to see, at the top of those stairs, a makeshift memorial made of ribbon and long-washed out crepe, swooping garlands of multi-colored nylon rope, and some plywood with painted hearts and initials on it similar to the tattoos Mary had on her legs.

"My son died two years back, and my daughter a few months ago. That's their memorial." She had stowed the water and was back to sweeping the sidewalk in front of her tent. "That's why I stay here."

We rarely learned anyone's whole story on the streets. The bits and pieces like Mary's reference, broom in hand, to her children, shot through my heart like one of the arrows in her tattoos. The permanence of her loss was inked on her body and also in the way that she lived. Once I understood about the memorial atop the slope behind her tent, it was hard to imagine her anywhere else.

My longing for a 2020-themed tattoo persisted well into 2021. Whatever I chose, once I could make up my mind and tattoo shops opened up, it would hold the confluence of many things: my leaving Seattle in favor of that strange little church, getting to the other side of the pandemic, and finding in myself more fight than I knew I had. I would certainly doubt myself again in the future, so why not put my hope and conviction in ink?

Perhaps—I thought to myself well into 2021—perhaps my 2020 tattoo would be words from the famous refrain to Cohen's song. But my words were not the ones most often quoted, especially in the weeks after Cohen's death in 2016: *There is a crack, a crack in everything/That's how the light gets in*. My words were the ones that came just before: *Forget your perfect offering*. If my experience had taught me anything it was that there is no such thing as a perfect offering. Radical hospitality taught me that. You can't expect perfection when you base a whole way of being on showing up with no solutions. You can't keep showing up with nothing more than your own deeply flawed humanity, and expect perfection. Mutual aid taught me there is no perfect offering. The church bell taught me that there is no perfect offering. Sometimes it rang, sometimes it didn't.

My post-2020 tattoo would be a bell. No words, no church cupola, no bright colors. I would know, though, all the stories that went into that bell. And every time I heard the church bell with its shallow clang-clang, I would think of all the people I'd met in the past year and in the past decades, people with whom I had shared hospitality, who had shared hospitality with me.

Celebrating Easter in the dark under a rented tent with a bunch of people who hadn't worshiped with other people for over a year taught me that there is no perfect offering. The church lawn itself was a study in flaw: up close, walking on it to set up chairs and hammer posts to support the tent, it was uneven to the point of being treacherous. Who can worry about a perfect offering when there are twisted ankles to worry about? But I was as stuck with that lawn as I was with my little parish. My choice to be there was the choice for the bumpy journey that lay ahead of us as much as the choice for that bumpy lawn no one had money or energy to fix.

Thirty-seven years after my baptism, on the Saturday before Easter in April 2021, I stood on that bumpy church lawn under a twenty-by-sixty-foot tent, asking the same questions Al had asked me: *Will you turn to Christ and accept him as your savior? Will you renounce the forces of evil?*

Will you strive for justice and peace, respecting every human being? Break bread and pray?

This was not a Saturday afternoon gathering of church ladies and baptism candidates but forty friends, musicians, congregation members, and a couple of retired clergy, all hungry for in-person church. It was our first gathering since early March of 2020. I had to shout over the traffic on 82nd Avenue; people answered in English and in Spanish: *I will, with God's help. Así lo haré, con el auxilio de Dios.* I prayed over a bowl of water the same prayers I'd heard for the first time all those years ago:

> *We thank you, Almighty God, for the gift of water.*
> *Over it the Holy Spirit moved in the beginning of creation.*

This time, the words were almost as familiar as my own name. I'd said them hundreds of times over water about to be used to baptize babies or adults, and, as on that night, to sprinkle over a gathered community recommitting themselves. Because of restrictions still in place, I couldn't actually sprinkle the people in the way I liked, big cedar branches loaded with water, enough to make mascara run and hair frizz. A single fir branch lay on the side of the silver bowl as I said the prayers, and I dipped it gingerly into the water and flung the branch to my right and left and behind me, hallowing the grass we stood on. That was the best we were going to do.

The same night I watered the grass with holy water, the people gathered were about to share communion together for the first time in over a year. My husband baked communion bread, using a recipe we'd used at other churches. There were four loaves; the number of people gathered could have been fed on one, but I loved the abundance signified by the big pile of bread on the altar in front of me. *The body of Christ; the bread of heaven.* As people came up for communion one by one, six feet apart, I pressed a thumb-sized hunk of bread into their hand. In other times I used to do that for people I recognized but were not regular churchgoers, and it was like a little private joke: *I'm giving you extra bread because I know you might not be here again for a long time.* This was different. None of us had been there for a long time. We all had a lot of communion bread to make up for.

In the old days, before the year of no Eucharist, there were two kinds of people: people who made eye contact with the priest while receiving their wafer or piece of bread, and people who looked down, focusing on the bread itself, or the floor, I never knew which. But on that Easter Eve, everyone locked eyes with me when I gave them their bread.

As people put away instruments, moved chairs back inside, and visited with people they hadn't seen in a year or more, I reflected on the evening. The music, planned and rehearsed for weeks, was amazing. A member of the Oregon Symphony brought her violin to play the haunting melody of the Lakota tune *Many and great*. Guitars and drums accompanied a lively rendition of *Resucitò* (Resurrected!*)* right after the lights came on and everyone rang tiny hand bells I'd placed under the chairs.

As I looked at the big pile of bread left over, I thought about all the people who weren't there. One parishioner had died a few months ago. Others were hale and hearty but didn't like to drive at night or hadn't been vaccinated yet and weren't quite ready to venture out, even fully masked. There were also people I wished were there from the neighborhood. For months, I had dreamed of a big gathering with food and music, but we weren't there yet. I missed Mark L-O-V-E, the guy with bright blue eyes who lived in his truck and used to show up on Tuesdays for dinner. No one had seen him for months. I thought about Mitch and Heather, whom I always thought of as the holy family. I saw Mitch every week, but he'd reported that Heather's mental state had deteriorated to the point that she never left her tent. I wondered when all the Crisis Kitchen volunteers might take me up on my invitation to join us on the lawn for worship sometime. I imagined bringing some bread to Mary as she swept outside her tent. I wondered about Sandy, with whom I'd shared a square of thickly frosted cake a few months earlier, and whether she would like to share that bread with us under the tent. I imagined my father at the edge of the crowd, taking it in.

Some of these people would be there next time, or the time after that. Some would never get there. Like the trajectory of the coronavirus, it was one of those things I didn't know.

Later that night as I was reflecting on the fullness of the evening: the friends who came, the music, the feeling of open space, not just on the lawn but in all of our hopes, I remembered that I hadn't rung the church bell. No one had.

I both hated and loved the imperfection of that. There was something so right about that detail not going nearly as planned. I knew that it would ring in the future, marking celebration and lament for the church and the neighborhood. I suspected the bell would probably break again, be repaired again, and ring again.